Improving the Performance of Governing Boards

by
Richard P. Chait
Thomas P. Holland
Barbara E. Taylor

AMERICAN COUNCIL ON EDUCATION ★
ORYX PRESS ★
Series on Higher Education
1996

© 1996 by the American Council on Education and The Oryx Press
Published by The Oryx Press
4041 North Central at Indian School Road
Phoenix, Arizona 85012-3397

Published simultaneously in Canada
Printed and bound in the United States of America
01   5 4

∞ The paper used in this publication meets the minimum requirements of the American National Standard for Information Sciences—Permanence of Paper for Printed Library Materials, ANSI Z39.48-1984.

Library of Congress Cataloging-in-Publication Data

Chait, Richard.
    Improving the performance of governing boards / by Richard P.
Chait, Thomas P. Holland, Barbara E. Taylor.
        p. cm. — (American Council on Education/Oryx Press series on
higher education)
    Includes bibliographical references (p.) and index.
    ISBN 1-57356-037-5 (alk. paper)
    1. College trustees—United States—Case studies.   2. Universities
and colleges—United States—Administration—Case studies.
3. Action research in education—United States.   I. Holland, Thomas
P. II. Taylor, Barbara E. III. Title. IV. Series.
LB2342.5C436   1996
378.1'011—dc20   96-39056
                                                    CIP

To my parents, Sara and David Chait,
for their steadfast love,
which has been a North Star on my journey through life.
—*Richard P. Chait*

To my wife, Myra Blackmon,
who provided invaluable support and encouragement
throughout all these efforts.
—*Thomas P. Holland*

To my mother, Mary Louise Taylor,
and to the memory of my father, Lowell C. Taylor,
who made everything possible.
—*Barbara E. Taylor*

CONTENTS

• • • • • • • • •

EXHIBITS

• • • • • • • • •

PREFACE

· · · · · · · · ·

T
he lineage of this book can be traced to the publication in 1991 of
The Effective Board of Trustees, which we also wrote together. That
book was largely motivated by one question: "Are there certain behaviors that characterize the most effective boards of trustees?" After three years
of research, we answered the question affirmatively. In fact, we identified six
distinct skill sets or competencies (summarized here in Chapter 1) that
differentiated strong boards from weak boards. This competency-based approach to governance was well received by trustees and administrators across
the not-for-profit sector, and by academic colleagues as well. In fact, the model
proved to be equally applicable to independent schools, hospitals, social
service agencies, and arts organizations. Wiser researchers might have quit
while ahead of the game, but we were beset by a new question: "Can boards of
trustees learn to improve, to become more competent?" In effect, we wanted
to move from theory to practice.

THE TRUSTEE DEMONSTRATION PROJECT

To answer this question, we designed an action research study, the Trustee
Demonstration Project, funded by the Lilly Endowment, to work closely and
collaboratively for five years with the boards of six independent colleges. We
began the project by issuing letters of inquiry to the presidents of 150 independent colleges in the eastern and central time zones. (Campuses farther west
were not considered because of greater travel time and costs.) Of the 150, 59
expressed interest in the project. After telephone interviews with the presidents of those institutions, 15 withdrew. We further pared the list to 13, based

upon 3 major factors: (1) the motivations of the president and the board chair to participate; we eliminated sites where the uppermost goals were either to raise money or to "clean house"; (2) a decision rule that excluded any college in the throes of an organizational crisis; and (3) the value, for research purposes, of ensuring some diversity among the institutions.

Based on these factors, we rank-ordered the institutions and arranged to conduct site visits at the first six colleges. On each campus, we met with the president, the chair of the board, between two and four other key trustees, a faculty leader, and the proposed staff liaison to the project. Our conversations concerned the board's motives, expectations, and commitment to the project, and the particular challenges the college faced. In all, we visited seven sites. As a result of this process, the following institutions were selected to participate in the project: Butler University (Indianapolis, Indiana), Cornell College (Mt. Vernon, Iowa), Eckerd College (St. Petersburg, Florida), Lane College (Jackson, Tennessee),[1] Randolph-Macon Woman's College (Lynchburg, Virginia), and the University of Findlay (Findlay, Ohio).

Once the sites had been selected, we wanted to ascertain the current competency level of each board. To do so we first conducted hour-long interviews with the president, the incumbent and the immediate past board chair, and five or six other key trustees. The interview protocol, identical to the earlier study (Chait, Holland, and Taylor 1991), elicited descriptive accounts of the board's behaviors. The three members of the research team then separately coded and scored each interview. In addition, we administered to all board members a self-assessment questionnaire (Exhibit 2.6), also geared to the competency-based model. From these sources, we were able to gauge the performance level of each board on each competency at that point in time.

Next, we established a three- to four-person liaison committee on each campus, which always included the president of the college and the board chair, to work with the project site director. With this committee, we planned an overnight retreat to present the model, to discuss the initial assessments, and to develop together a customized work plan to strengthen areas of lesser competency at that point in time.

While the particulars at each site differed, there were a few commonalities. Almost every trustee was congenial, but many were initially disconcerted by the "academic" and "theoretical" nature of the model. Most were disappointed by their board's lower-than-expected scores, and all opted to work most diligently on the educational dimension (see Exhibit 1.1 in Chapter 1), the area where scores were uniformly the lowest.

The heart of the project occurred subsequent to the retreat. For the next 36 months, the designated project site director visited the campus at least twice a year and also conversed regularly by telephone with the board chair and/or the president, trustee officers, and senior staff. We observed the board and trustee committees in operation, provided written and oral commentaries on the board's performance, and recommended various tools and techniques to improve the board's competency. Sometimes a board adapted a generic idea to meet local circumstances or invented a new approach. In all cases, the board and the president decided which recommendations (if any) to pursue. We offered suggestions and feedback—we did not issue directives.

As the project proceeded, the sites became more self-aware and therefore more self-sufficient. Consequently, we receded. The role of the site director gradually and deliberately shifted from outside expert to internal coach. More and more, we became observers, counselors, and occasionally troubleshooters.

Once a year, we held a "summit" session, a one-day meeting that convened the board chairs and presidents from all sites. These occasions afforded each leadership team the opportunity to share with one another their experiences, successes, and setbacks; to set goals for the next 12 months; and to advise the project team about the strengths and weaknesses of the interventions. Without exception, the participants rated the summit sessions as among the most valuable components of the project.

In the later stages of the study, the formal interviews were repeated, although this time the questions were posed by professionals unaffiliated with the project in order to encourage the most candid responses. The interviews were again independently coded and scored, and the self-assessment questionnaire was readministered.[2] Finally, we debriefed each project site either at a second retreat or as part of a regularly scheduled board meeting.

We have included this description of the project primarily as background information and not to suggest that every board intent on self-improvement needs to mount a comparably elaborate effort. This book distills the best practices and the most important lessons that emerged from the demonstration project precisely so that trustees and presidents of other institutions do not have to undertake an intensive, five-year engagement with a team of researchers to become a better board.

Boards of trustees can benefit immediately and significantly from the experiences, experiments, successes, and missteps of the project sites. We suggest no policies or practices that are not already operative with one or more boards. Many of the lessons that we learned and many of the stories and suggestions that we relate are drawn from 20 or so other colleges, schools, and nonprofit organizations where we have acted, usually on a short-term basis, as consultants to the board. At the very least, then, readers can be assured that all the recommendations and innovations that we present here have been field tested in real-life environments. Whenever possible throughout the text, we have allowed the "voices" of individuals from both the project and consultation sites to speak directly because their stories, insights, and perceptions are so powerfully instructive.

RELEVANCE TO NONPROFIT ORGANIZATIONS BEYOND HIGHER EDUCATION

Concurrent with the Lilly project, Professor Holland initiated a companion study, funded by the Kellogg Foundation. In virtually every respect, the projects were parallel except that the Kellogg sites included social service and health care agencies, as well as institutions of higher education. The Kellogg project participants were: the Atlanta (Georgia) Chapter of the Alzheimer's Association, Clara Maas Health Care System (Belleville, New Jersey), Frisbee Hospital (Rochester, New Hampshire), Notre Dame College (Manchester, New Hampshire), United Way of Greater Nashua (New Hampshire), and Virginia Commonwealth University (Richmond).

We believe strongly that the relevance of the experiences and the usefulness of the conclusions presented here apply throughout the not-for-profit sector. While each and every nonprofit organization stakes a claim to be unique (which is at least one trait they all have in common), the central elements of effective governance, as described in Chapter 1, are really quite generic.

Although the essence of governance does not differ greatly across the not-for-profit sector, the vocabulary does. Therefore, readers less familiar with higher education might bear in mind these "translations":

> college, university, or institution = organization or agency
> board of trustees = board of directors
> president = executive director, school head, or CEO
> faculty = professional staff
> students = consumers, clients, or patients

ORGANIZATION OF THE BOOK

We have organized this book around the governance concerns most frequently raised by trustees. Therefore, the most logical way to provide an overview of the contents of the book may be to list the major questions that shaped each chapter.

Chapter 1
- What is effective trusteeship and why is it so difficult to realize?
- In what ways do boards most add value to the institutions they govern and what skills underlie this achievement?

Chapter 2
- How does an institution start and sustain the process of board development?
- How can the board's performance be evaluated and monitored?

Chapter 3
- How does a collection of trustees become an effective and well-organized board?
- What roles should be played by the board's leaders and by the institution's CEO?

Chapter 4
- What does a board need to know to be effective?
- How can boards best acquire that knowledge?

Chapter 5
- How can boards maintain a strategic focus?
- How can boards do business better; that is, have more consequential meetings illuminated by more meaningful information?

Chapter 6
- What are the reasons trustees and presidents resist board development and what are the counterarguments?
- What are the payoffs from board development?

ACKNOWLEDGMENTS

We were extraordinarily blessed throughout the course of this work to enjoy the financial support of the Lilly Endowment and the Kellogg Foundation and the moral support of Ralph Lundgren and Robert DeVries, program officers at the Endowment and the Foundation, respectively. Richard Chait and Barbara Taylor also benefitted from sabbaticals provided by, respectively, the University of Maryland at College Park and the Association of Governing Boards of Universities and Colleges.

On the Kellogg project, Professor Anthony Kovner of New York University and Dean Roger Ritvo of the University of New Hampshire ably played the lead role with the health care organizations. We also benefitted immensely from the unusually conscientious and industrious efforts of three graduate students: Lori Potts-Dupre and Merrill Schwartz at the University of Maryland and Douglas Jackson at the University of Georgia. Toward the end of the project, site interviews were conducted by Ms. Potts-Dupre and Ms. Schwartz, as well as by David Boyle, Karen Grochau, Robert Myers, and Nike Speltz. Kay Giannuzzi at Maryland and Martha Lund at Georgia, both exceptionally capable, were indispensable to the projects' administrative and clerical operations.

We have learned a great deal from a great many colleagues, too many to cite individually. We do, however, want to recognize collectively the valuable and insightful conversations we have had over the years with associates at The Cheswick Center, and with fellow trustees of Goucher College and Maryville College (Richard Chait) and Wittenberg University (Barbara Taylor), where we have been privileged to serve as board members.

Most of all, though, we want to express our deepest gratitude to the trustees and administrators of the sites that were associated with these projects. Despite our nominal roles as coaches and "experts," we are convinced that we learned far more from these boards than we imparted.

Since academics and others sometimes make too much of the order in which the authors' names appear, we wish to note that we were equal partners in this endeavor. The sequence of names was determined solely by the sequence of the alphabet.

NOTES

1. Lane College withdrew during the first year of the project after the sudden death of its president.

2. For a complete technical report on preproject and postproject results, see Holland, Taylor, Chait, and Jackson, "Measuring the Performance of Governing Boards" (1996). Some key findings are summarized in Chapter 6 of this volume.

CHAPTER

Swimming against the Tide

A fter 10 years of research and dozens of engagements as consultants to nonprofit boards, we have reached a rather stark conclusion: *effective governance by a board of trustees is a relatively rare and unnatural act.*

We mean no disrespect by this statement. Most trustees are bright and earnest individuals. However, the tides of trusteeship carry boards in the wrong direction: from strategy toward operations, from long-term challenges toward immediate concerns, from collective action toward individual initiatives. In order to add significant value and afford the institution a competitive advantage, boards must constantly swim against the currents.

Unless counterforces are initiated and sustained, the board will not achieve effective governance, defined here as *a collective effort, through smooth and suitable processes, to take actions that advance a shared purpose consistent with the institution's mission.*

Regrettably, most boards just drift with the tides. As a result, trustees are often little more than high-powered, well-intentioned people engaged in low-level activities. The board dispatches an agenda of potpourri tied tangentially at best to the organization's strategic priorities and central challenges.

We did not reach this judgment alone. Most trustees whom we encountered were quick to acknowledge dissatisfaction and disillusionment with their board's performance. From hundreds of interviews and conversations that we had with board members and senior staff, cited throughout this book, four standard complaints emerged:

1. "There's no red meat on the table." The issues before the board and its committees are little more than a mishmash of miscellany; trivial matters disconnected from one another and from corporate strategy.

2. "Board meetings are boring." Events are tightly scripted, outcomes are largely predetermined, and opportunities to substantially influence significant decisions are severely limited.
3. "We have plenty of information, but we have no idea what it all means." Board packets bulge with raw, uninterpreted data, and trustees suffer from a deluge, not a dearth, of information.
4. "The parts on this board sum to less than the whole." The trustees' individual talents are not harnessed to a collective effort. The board functions more like foursomes on the same golf course than like players on the same team. Each committee or clique engages in a self-contained event on a common terrain, largely oblivious to the activities of others.

Taken together, these conditions leave many trustees disheartened: "My presence at board meetings is basically immaterial to the outcome." "Sometimes when I get back on the plane after a meeting, I think, 'Why did I come? I did not make any major contribution.'" The board as a whole typically performs below capacity and, from an institutional perspective, a potentially valuable asset goes underutilized. "We are like accomplished musicians unable to play a symphony together," observed one trustee.

WHY DO BOARDS UNDERPERFORM?

In *The Corporate Board*, Demb and Neubauer describe three "structural tensions that beset all boards and that reflect basic paradoxes characteristic of the board setting" (1992, 5). The paradoxes, paraphrased (ibid., 4–7), are:

1. The board has clear legal responsibility for the corporation, yet management has the infrastructure, knowledge, time, and appetite to bear this responsibility.
2. The board must be sufficiently independent and detached to render critical judgments, yet at the same time, directors identify with the company and bond with the executive officers—a closeness that can compromise or cloud objectivity.
3. The board must find a balance between a cozy club and a loosely linked group of feisty individualists.

While many people assume that corporate and nonprofit boards are radically different, we realized that nonprofit boards confront four fundamental difficulties that closely parallel the three paradoxes of the corporate board. Successful boards recognize that these difficulties are inherent tensions that can never be entirely resolved or eliminated. Instead, better boards develop an acute awareness of these impediments to effective governance and then strive to minimize and counteract the negative effects. What are the obstacles to greater nonprofit board effectiveness?

Obstacle 1: Dispassionate Analysts and Impassioned Advocates

Both professional staff and the literature on trusteeship consistently advise governing boards to be objective stewards. Trustees are expected to rise above parochial interests and personal biases in order to make decisions that are in the best interests of the long-term welfare of the institution.

At the same time, the professional staff want board members to be committed, psychologically and financially, to the institution. The trustees are encouraged to be ardent advocates and generous contributors; however, as the board's ardor intensifies, objectivity may decrease. There are, for instance, college and university boards composed predominantly of zealous alumni who behave more like the directors of a family-owned company than like analytical fiduciaries. More commonly, some trustees develop such fervent attachments to a particular department or program, or to a bygone era, that even the pretense of dispassionate analysis disappears.

This intrinsic tension between heartfelt affection and studied neutrality arises most frequently with respect to the board's relationship to the institution's president. On the one hand, the trustees must maintain some distance and detachment in order to evaluate the CEO's performance objectively. On the other hand, CEOs expect (and many boards desire) that trustees will be sympathetic colleagues and supportive friends—the CEO's principal source of nurturance.[1]

In short, boards constantly wrestle with when to be "product champions" and when to be studied neutrals—whether to stand and cheer like rabid partisans in Congress when the President of the United States delivers the State of the Union address, or to remain seated and stone faced like Supreme Court justices who may be called upon some day to decide the constitutionality of the matter at hand.

Obstacle 2: Part-time Amateurs and Full-time Professionals

In most cases, governing boards of nonprofit organizations are not composed of trustees who are experts in the institution's particular domain. From a trustee's perspective, the organization may resemble a foreign culture with different mores, strange customs, and odd values. As one member of a college board commented about the institution's practice of shared governance, "It's immobilizing. If I had to make a living doing this, I'd go nuts."

As part-time amateurs largely unfamiliar with the organization's culture, trustees are not especially well equipped to oversee the work of full-time professionals and to be the ultimate arbiters of a prudent course of action.[2] Without specialized knowledge (see Chapter 4), trustees tend to dwell on the more familiar realms of operations, finance, and investment, usually to the neglect of the institution's core business. "It's patently obvious," confessed one trustee, "that we don't know enough about these types of ventures to perform the duties of trustees."

In strange territory, trustees often choose between two well-worn paths. One leads trustees to defer uncritically to management; ironically, a tendency most often noted by senior administrators. "The board's still not very inquisitive about important topics. There's a tendency for them to be too polite," commented one president. A college vice president remarked, "The board doesn't challenge assumptions to the extent I would look for. Maybe it's because I'm inside higher education and they are outside and don't know what questions to ask. . . . Screw up your courage . . . ask the questions." Illustrative of this same problem, a current trustee and former college president explained, "It's not a problem of individual capability. Most trustees have had corporate board experiences, but they are baffled by the academic world. There is a lack of know-how about academic governance and how it should work."

The other path leads board members to force a more familiar corporate model on nonprofit institutions. In a comment that captures the attitude of many peers, one college trustee proclaimed that "a university must be run like a complex business." In a more extreme example of the same perspective, a university board member insisted, "You have to drop what doesn't sell. Why have classes in Medieval history if there are only a few students? I would offer anything that's legal and enrolls students." Another member of the same board concurred: "We should have a three- to five-percent rate of return, irrespective of events or the effect on morale or quality."

This entrepreneurial, capitalistic view might be contrasted with the definition of a university offered by the late A. Bartlett Giamatti (1988), then president of Yale.

> A college or university is an institution where financial incentives are absent; where the product line is not a unit or an object but rather a value-laden and life-long process; where the goal of the enterprise is not growth or market share but intellectual excellence; not profit or proprietary rights but the free good of knowledge . . . not increased productivity in economic terms but increased intensity of thinking. . . .

While many educators do not subscribe entirely to these views, the vast majority are more sympathetic to Giamatti's characterization of the university than to the notion of the "college as corporation." As long as there are such significant philosophical differences between academics and trustees on a college board (or comparable disagreements within other nonprofit organizations), the institution will be hard pressed to achieve effective governance.

Obstacle 3: All Stars and No Constellation

Ordinarily (and especially among independent nonprofit organizations), trustees are selected on the basis of demonstrated ability and achievement. Board members are, almost by definition, conspicuously successful and often powerful and influential individuals, accustomed to leadership roles. Nearly all trustees feel comfortable in the role of signal caller—someone able to scan the environment, assign responsibilities, and execute the play. Far fewer of them acclimate easily to the role of one among many constitutionally equal members of an entity that acts collectively.

In short, most boards of trustees resemble a huddle of quarterbacks. Large egos lurk inside almost every helmet. As one trustee observed about the institution's effort to "ratchet up" board membership, "As you bring on stronger people, they are more set in their ways. . . . With this new breed, they're just as creative and even more aggressive, and they have agendas they want to accomplish. The stronger the board members, the harder it is just to get them to meld into the group." In another instance, a trustee, asked to undertake a special assignment, set the terms as follows: "I made it clear that if I did so, I would have to have control and the power to act quickly. I wanted a very small group to work with me. You can't take time to keep everyone updated on every detail and still get the job done."

To compound the problem, most boards rarely practice as a team.[3] Trustees customarily meet to govern, not to rehearse. While such behavior would be catastrophic for a theater troupe, a ballet company, or an athletic squad, many board members see little need to enhance teamwork. Skeptical of the board's collective role or impact, self-confident and action-oriented trustees frequently prefer to act individually. Rather than attempting to sway the opinion of the board as a whole, such trustees will buttonhole or telephone the president of the institution or the board chair before—and sometimes even after—the board has deliberated, in order to influence the outcome on a particular issue. We have seen college and university trustees behave in this manner on matters that ranged from tuition and fees, to senior-level appointments, to the future of fraternities. As trustees move outside the context of *board* action, the institution's president or executive director, in effect, reports to more and more individuals and becomes increasingly susceptible to contradictory advice from strong-minded board members, ultimately an untenable position for a CEO.

We should note briefly that, among the college boards that we have studied or advised, this pattern was less evident at women's colleges where women constituted a majority of the members. One president of a women's college commented after about a year on campus, "What I haven't seen here that I have seen on other boards is a lot of personal agendas and large egos. They are not using the board as a personal platform. It's very refreshing." Likewise, a female trustee stated that "there may be less ego involved" among women board members. Her view was echoed by a male member of the same board: "Women are not yet prone to the male ego problems. . . . As they rise in the corporate world they may get big egos as the men do, but for the short term they don't seem to have as big egos."

Obstacle 4: Low Stakes and High Rollers

With rare exceptions (such as the United Way of America, whose former CEO misappropriated more than $1 million of organizational funds), there are few penalties for the sins of misgovernance, especially compared with the punishments attached to sins of mismanagement. Newspapers normally publish the CEO's picture—not the board's—beside an article on an institution's setbacks or crises. Legally, the board may be collectively responsible for the organization, but, in reality, individual trustees are virtually unaccountable. "Individual performance on the board is not something we talk about," acknowledged one trustee. A member of another board admitted, "It's nice to hold other people accountable, but then evade accountability ourselves. We have a clear list of what we expect from the president. Now we need to specify what we expect of ourselves." As a volunteer and as merely one board member among many, most trustees can avoid or minimize personal accountability. "It's not as if I am a general partner in a private firm with unlimited liability," declared a board committee chair.

Even if the institution falters, trustees can avert personal embarrassment and humiliation. As prominent citizens with an accumulation of "social credits" from successes in other venues, trustees are often presumed to be competent by other opinion leaders and are, therefore, granted the benefit of the doubt. Indeed, a trustee's resignation typically reflects poorly on the institution and not on the board member. Stated simply, the stakes for trustees individually are relatively low. Few board members lose much sleep over trusteeship, even though the caliber of governance that the trustees provide has profound consequences for the institution.

Despite the powerful currents and unfavorable odds, some boards succeed. Of the 29 boards that participated in our research projects, we classified 8 (plus a few consultancy sites) as particularly effective.[4] These might be considered the "benchmark" boards, the ones that set the standards of desirable performance. Why do these boards excel? What distinguishes exceptional boards from the others?

THE COMPETENCIES OF EFFECTIVE BOARDS

After site visits to 22 campuses, interviews with more than 110 trustees and college presidents, and self-assessment survey responses from over 400 board members, we identified in 1991 6 distinct competencies that undergirded the actual behaviors of demonstrably effective boards of trustees. These six skill sets provided the framework for the current Trustee Demonstration Project. Indeed, the central goal of the project was to strengthen the boards' abilities along these six dimensions of effective trusteeship.

The Effective Board of Trustees (Chait, Holland, and Taylor 1991) describes each competency at length (one per chapter). Therefore, we will only summarize the basic elements of each skill set (see Exhibit 1.1) and note slight modifications to two competencies based upon experiences with the Trustee Demonstration Project sites.

The Competencies of Effective Governing Boards

Contextual Dimension

The board understands and takes into account the culture and norms of the organization it governs. The board:

- Adapts to the distinctive characteristics and culture of the institution's environment.
- Relies on the institution's mission, values, and tradition as a guide for decisions.
- Acts so as to exemplify and reinforce the organization's values.

Educational Dimension

The board takes the necessary steps to ensure that trustees are knowledgeable about the institution, the profession, and the board's roles, responsibilities, and performance. The board:

- Consciously creates opportunities for trustee education and development.
- Regularly seeks information and feedback on its own performance.
- Pauses periodically for self-reflection, to diagnose its strengths and limitations, and to examine its mistakes.

Interpersonal Dimension

The board nurtures the development of trustees as a working group, attends to the board's collective welfare, and fosters a sense of cohesiveness. The board:

- Creates a sense of inclusiveness among trustees.
- Develops groups goals and recognizes group achievements.
- Identifies and cultivates leadership within the board.

Analytical Dimension

The board recognizes the complexities and subtleties of issues and accepts ambiguity and uncertainty as healthy preconditions for critical discussion. The board:

- Approaches matters from a broad institutional outlook.
- Dissects and examines all aspects of multifaceted issues.
- Raises doubts, explores tradeoffs, and encourages the expression of differences of opinion.

EXHIBIT 1.1

continued

Political Dimension

The board accepts as a primary responsibility the need to develop and maintain healthy relationships among major constituencies. The board:

- Respects the integrity of the governance process and the legitimate roles and responsibilities of other stakeholders.
- Consults often and communicates directly with key constituencies.
- Attempts to minimize conflict and win/lose situations.

Strategic Dimension

The board helps the institution envision a direction and shape a strategy. The board:

- Cultivates and concentrates on processes that sharpen institutional priorities.
- Organizes itself and conducts its business in light of the institution's strategic priorities.
- Anticipates potential problems, and acts before issues become crises.
- Anticipates potential problems, and acts before matters become urgent.

EXHIBIT 1.1 (continued)

The competencies can be divided into two groups. The contextual, educational, analytical, and strategic dimensions are essentially *cognitive* skills; all four involve the board's capacity to learn, analyze, decide, and act. The interpersonal and political dimensions concern *affective* or relational skills, oriented more toward process than substance. Not unexpectedly, we discovered that boards value more and perform better the cognitive skills. Trustees are more comfortable with context, information, analysis, and strategy than with the board's internal dynamics or the institution's political climate. Nonetheless, all are important to effective trusteeship.

Based on the Trustee Demonstration Project, we have concluded that the competency-based model works, especially as a means to diagnose and analyze board behavior and to evaluate a board's performance. At the same time, we learned from experience that the definitions of the interpersonal and analytical dimensions needed to be modified slightly.

With respect to the interpersonal skill set, we originally focused too much on the social relationships among trustees outside the boardroom and on the degree of friendliness manifested inside the boardroom. We became sidetracked by whether trustees dined, socialized, played, or travelled with one another. A more accurate conceptualization of the interpersonal dimension would emphasize inclusiveness within the board as opposed to friendship outside the board. In other words, boards skilled in this area assure trustees of their unconditional membership—equal opportunity to participate, obtain information, and influence events, and the confidence to be critical without fear of recrimination or isolation. A few concrete examples of competency in this dimension include: informal lunches hosted by the board chair and the institution's president to ensure that trustees are comfortable with the board's operations, participation by all trustees in the orientation of new members, and a conference call by the president and the chair after every board meeting to update absent trustees. Telltale signs to the contrary include the reality or perception of an inner circle of power within the board (often, though not always, the executive committee) or the partition of the board into social or ideological factions.

The analytical dimension, as originally stated, encapsulated the board's capacity to analyze problems and process information from multiple perspectives. In fact, we first labelled this the intellectual dimension. We now believe that the definition should emphasize the acceptance of ambiguity and uncertainty *as healthy preconditions for comprehensive and critical discussions.* Boards with analytical competency are much more likely to raise doubts, explore the downside, and address tradeoffs. Issues are on the table, open to analysis and to discussion. Conflicts of opinion are welcome, even encouraged through small group discussions or multiconstituency task forces. On less competent boards, on the other hand, the staff and trustees present information, reports, and recommendations with such certainty and conviction as to chill debate. Presidents are expected to present perfect solutions to knotty problems. Trustees are expected to dutifully endorse committee recommendations with little or no conversation or dissent.

With these modifications, we are more convinced than ever that the six competencies are *the* skill sets that a board must possess to govern ably. At the same time, we (and members of exemplary boards) recognize that competent boards and effective governance have only marginal utility unless these assets engender decisions and actions that add value to the institution, which should, of course, be the ultimate goal of any governing body.

ADDING VALUE

When academics contemplate the most important gift a board could bestow upon a college or a university, images of six- or seven-figure checks almost certainly come to mind. While we hardly want to denigrate the value of such munificence, the most effective boards make an even more valuable contribution: decisions and actions that enhance the long-term quality, vitality, and stability of the institution. In short, the best boards add the most value—usually through five interrelated approaches.

Approach 1: Help Senior Management Determine What Matters Most

Effective boards identify, with the executive staff, the most significant institutional issues that will require the attention of the trustees and senior managers. For example, the board of trustees of Duke University recently devoted a two-day retreat chiefly to a discussion and analysis of the greatest opportunities and most worrisome vulnerabilities on the horizon. At another institution, heavily dependent upon government grants, the board and the president decided together that no item should command more attention than inventing the future of the post–federally funded research university.

Sometimes presidents or CEOs are reluctant to tackle certain crucial issues that are too controversial, outside the scope of their central interests, or beyond the comfort level of their expertise. In other instances, the board may have a broader exposure and, therefore, a keener appreciation for the imperative to act; for example, on initiatives related to technology, globalization, or strategic alliances with industry. In both cases, the board must motivate, prod, or direct the CEO to attend to the matter.

Without discipline, however, boards sometimes unintentionally convey the message that "everything matters most." The problem usually arises because different trustees have different views (a potentially healthy condition) that are never reconciled (a potentially dangerous condition). Consequently, the board's deliberations end with mixed messages or a "Mission Impossible."

"It was helpful when some trustees would let me, as president, know what they expected, but then the expectations were often inconsistent or contradictory. . . . The chairman should have demanded that the board come together and speak with one voice."

We have watched undisciplined college boards of trustees conclude that the quality, quantity, and diversity of students should simultaneously be increased despite adverse market conditions, or that both deferred maintenance and depressed faculty salaries should be remedied without substantial tuition increases, or that the faculty should be more dedicated to undergraduate education and intensify efforts to enhance revenues through sponsored research, executive education, and technology transfer.

To cite an especially instructive example, the board of an independent liberal arts college charged a four-person ad hoc committee to conduct an evaluation of the president's first year that included conversations with most trustees and all of the vice presidents. Almost everyone had only one criticism of an otherwise enormously successful start: the president was overextended and overscheduled. However, neither the ad hoc committee nor the board ever discussed where the president's commitments might be reduced. The development committee needed the president on the road for the capital campaign, the academic affairs committee believed that the president's presence on campus was essential to restore the faculty's deflated morale, the student affairs committee wanted the president to be highly accessible and visible to students, and so on. In the end, the president was not so much without the trustees' opinions—many board members commented privately or extended an invitation that tacitly conveyed a personal preference—as without the trustees' guidance. The president did not have a clear sense of the board's will, a pointed reminder that boards add more value when trustees expressly agree on *relative* priorities; on what matters most.

Approach 2: Create Opportunities for the President to Think Aloud

We have never encountered a board that did not appreciate the pivotal role of the institution's president or executive director. (If anything, a few boards overestimate the CEO's impact.) Indeed, many trustees believe that the board bears no greater, and sometimes no other, responsibility than to "hire and fire" the president.

In light of the importance trustees attach to presidents, we are continually surprised that so few boards create situations in which the CEO can reflect and ruminate with the board. In many ways, the ultimate contribution that a board makes to an institution may be shaping or refining the president's thinking. If that is the case, then the more chances the president has to expose his or her thinking to the trustees, the more chances the trustees have to add value.

As a rule, there are regular opportunities for the president to provide progress reports and other factual updates to the board. Similarly, presidential recommendations are usually accompanied by a statement of rationale. To be sure, these moments offer trustees a glimpse of the president's priorities and concerns. But how often are there occasions for the president to muse about a concern, to sketch a dream, or to test an embryonic idea? If a decision has to be made about whether to allocate time to listen to the president's report or to listen to the president's reflections, the choice seems obvious.

Whether at a "president's hour," an executive session (see Chapter 5), or as part of an extended discussion of preliminary plans or tentative notions, the board should provide the forum and create the atmosphere where a president can speak freely, securely, and intimately.[5] If it is truly lonely at the top, where else can CEOs turn, if not to the board, to unburden themselves? Among the topics that have been presented by college presidents and mulled by their boards in this manner were: tensions among senior administrators, disaffection among alumni, speculation about a radically new future for the college that involved a possible merger, concerns about personal burnout, the intractable dilemma of student financial aid, the role of athletics, the place of fraternities, and the implications of factional disputes within the sponsoring religious denomination.

Some trustees may contend that most of these matters should be presented to the board or a trustee committee in the context of a policy recommendation. However, that misses the point. The discussion is *not* intended to formulate policy. Rather, the principal purposes are to enable the president to frame problems; to contemplate the basic values, tradeoffs, and ambiguities that underlie and may eventually inform a policy recommendation; and to benefit from the informal counsel of respected and trusted board members precisely at a time when neither the problem nor the solution has been conclusively defined.

A board of trustees cannot add value as a "sounding board" unless the board takes ample soundings. It is as simple as that.

Approach 3: Encourage Experimentation

A board should act as a stimulus for change. We do not wish to underestimate the task. As Donald Kennedy, former president of Stanford University, eloquently explains the challenge:

> Leadership *can* be exercised, but it has significant limitations. . . .
> [T]enure, disciplinary loyalty, the structure of academic politics, monumental physical arrangements, and investment patterns create huge regret functions—favor a stability that may be very useful in some ways, but makes it difficult for the university to take new directions nimbly. It enhances a distribution of decision-making power in which the periphery has a clear advantage over the center. (Kennedy 1994, 93, 98)

Surely, the board (and the president) of a college or university are part of the "center" and thus at a relative disadvantage, especially with respect to changes in academic programs as opposed to shifts in administrative practices. Nevertheless, we have observed boards that add substantial value as instruments for change and reform.

Often these occasions to stimulate change arose at board retreats (see Chapter 2) purposefully designed to nudge the trustees and the institution toward more creative and original thinking. In almost every instance, we should note, professional staff participated in these retreats, a symbolic and substantive recognition of the key role they play in change strategies. Among the assignments that moved the participants to be imaginative were:

- Conduct a mental tour of the campus 10 years from today. Note the most visible and tangible signs that the college successfully adapted to the most significant environmental forces for change evident today.
- Describe where the institution should be five years from now in the eyes of its key constituencies.
- Discuss the results of a survey that asked trustees and senior staff to identify what will and what should be most different about the institution in 10 years.
- On the assumption that money does not matter, identify the one or two most promising initiatives or actions the institution could take in the next two years to markedly improve its standing and/or the quality of services it offers.

• Imagine that the institution were a for-profit business. What would the staff and the board do differently?

While these exercises might strike some trustees as academic and impractical, most, in fact, produced the germs of ideas that have been pursued further and even implemented. Among these innovations at the colleges and universities we studied were a new international campus, strategic alliances with nearby colleges, the outsourcing of certain administrative services and operations, a reconfiguration of the curriculum around the concept of leadership, greater emphasis on learning partnerships, experiential learning, career links at a liberal arts college, and a redefinition of a college's mission to incorporate a more active role as a voice for women in America.

In some cases, change arises because the board sets limits that, in effect, force change. The board of one distinguished college placed a cap on the number of full-time equivalent faculty, which effectively required the faculty to accept the proposition of "growth by substitution." Another trustee committee linked any growth in the overall size of the faculty to a stipulation that all vacancies were returned to the provost for redistribution to the program with the greatest strategic claim on additional personnel.

In other instances, the seeds of change arose from little more than insightful questions by trustees. When plans were presented for a new science center at an independent school, the physical plant committee of one institution wondered, "Will science in the 21st century occur in a building?" While plans for the facility have not been scrubbed, the question did precipitate a reconsideration of the design. Likewise, a trustee of a college handicapped by a remote, rural location asked, "Why do we need a campus at all, given today's technology?" The response was not to abandon the campus but to plan a trial foray into distance learning.

To encourage experimentation, then, boards should think creatively with faculty and staff, set policies that require conscious choices and explicit tradeoffs, and sometimes raise counterintuitive and iconoclastic questions. In addition, boards eager to promote responsible risk should create a safe environment for faculty and staff to falter on occasion.

Approach 4: Monitor Progress and Performance

It is difficult to imagine a corporate board that does not monitor the company's financial and strategic performance on a regular and routine basis. Indeed, corporate directors have been chided from time to time for being too concerned with the "bottom line." By contrast, the boards of nonprofit organizations are generally not quite so vigilant. "Corporate boards devote much more time to reviews of performance (short-term and long-term) than do boards of nonprofits," observes William Bowen (1994, 24), president of the Andrew W. Mellon Foundation, former president of Princeton University, and an outside director of several Fortune 500 corporations. "The boards of nonprofits," Bowen continues, "are notoriously subject to the problem of failing to see a fast, clearly visible train coming—even when it is moving inexorably and their organization is sitting right on the tracks."

The difference between corporate and collegiate boards on this score can largely be explained by the lack of knowledge and lack of agreement among trustees about the appropriate performance metrics for higher education. While responsible for the long-term welfare of the institution, the average board seems unsure about how to monitor progress and measure results, especially beyond the realms of finance, investment, and construction. And even where the indicators are known, trustees are not certain how to interpret the results. Is it desirable, for example, to be the lowest-cost provider within a peer group, or to realize a notable increase in the students' overall grade point average, or to achieve a nominal productivity gain through a one-week reduction in the length of the semester?

In Chapter 4, we describe a mechanism, the "dashboard," and suggest some specific performance indicators that enable a board to monitor a college's condition. We want to emphasize here that the board's concern should extend beyond operations to all key elements of policy and strategy. How normal— and yet how odd—that the board of one of the nation's finest universities recently adopted a strategic plan without any explicit benchmarks, mileposts, or yardsticks to gauge results. If the strategic initiatives were, hypothetically, to increase entrepreneurship, international activity, the quality of under-graduate education, and service to society, then the board should insist that the plan specify the means, criteria, and standards to chart progress on a defined timetable and against stated norms.

Without establishing a means to monitor the plan and assess its effective-ness, the board had not added as much value as possible to the fulfillment of the institution's strategy. The board of trustees of a liberal arts college offered a more useful response, albeit under very different circumstances. The faculty asserted in a letter to the board that the "quality of education and the quality of the faculty here has slipped badly" as a result of an allegedly heavy-handed administration. The missive prompted the board's academic affairs committee to ask that the faculty identify the indices that were used to assess the quality of the education and the faculty. A productive series of discussions ensued. Some policies and practices were modified but, more important, the institu-tion now had an agreed upon set of measures to assess whether the improve-ments that the faculty anticipated as a result of these changes, in fact, materialized.

The same principle applies across the spectrum of policy decisions. If a university's administration proposes a new merit-based compensation plan to motivate performance and to retain the best faculty, how will the institution know whether the system worked? If policies are enacted to increase employee morale, faculty-student interactions, or the quality of the students' first-year experience, how will the results be measured and how can we determine cause and effect?

When boards mandate that questions such as these be answered, there are two positive effects. First, the faculty and the administration must, in fact, define the dimensions of success. Second, the board has a built-in means to determine whether an adopted policy has achieved the intended objectives and whether any mid-course adjustments are warranted. The board, in short, has a way to see *and avoid* "a fast, clearly visible train coming."

Approach 5: Model the Desired Behaviors

A colloquialism popular today urges leaders "to walk the walk and not just talk the talk." In other words, leaders are expected to personify the organization's values and goals. This advice may be particularly appropriate in higher education where faculty and students appear to be innately cynical and genetically equipped to detect even the slightest aroma of hypocrisy. Unfortunately, a good many boards of trustees are vulnerable to the charge of inconsistency, if not insincerity.

Most boards of nonprofits these days contain a rather large and vocal chorus of trustees convinced that one or another modern management technique should be instituted. The candidates include, among others, Total Quality Management (TQM), Continuous Quality Improvement (CQI), Business Process Reengineering (BPR), and some old chestnuts like Quality Control Circles, Management by Objectives (MBO), and Zero Base Budgeting (ZBB). Ironically, as avidly as some trustees tout the benefits of such approaches, these very concepts have not been seriously embraced and widely applied to the board's work. In fact, as noted in Chapter 3, boards cling to traditional trustee committees as obstinately as faculty hold to conventional academic departments, even though much might be gained on both fronts from "reinvented" structures.

Similarly, college trustees may call for the institution to downsize the faculty, eliminate the deadwood, abolish tenure, and increase productivity. The boardroom analog to these pleas are obvious: reduce the size of the board, deny reappointments to incapable trustees, impose term limits on board members, and add more value as a board. In reality, most faculties and most boards resist these reforms, usually for the same reasons: fear of change, limited energy, preservation of self-interest, doubts about the cost-benefit ratio, and concern for the sensibilities of others. In other words, boards of trustees cannot be both the champions of change and the personification of the status quo.

Trustees add value when the board leads the way through example, and not merely through pronouncements. At one of our project sites, the entire board participates every year in a day of public service to underscore the college's commitment to the community. On another campus where all academic departments and all administrative units are reviewed by outside examiners every five years, the trustees commissioned an external evaluation of the board on the same timetable to stress that the trustees had the same commitment to rigor and no intention to assert an exemption from the process. In a third instance, the trustees mounted a vigorous campaign to diversify the composition of the board concurrent with the approval of a strategic initiative to diversify the faculty and the staff.

Each of these efforts to align the trustees' behavior with organizational values and institutional policies attracted the attention and admiration of faculty, students, and staff. More significantly, the trustees added considerable value because the boards' symbolic actions smoothed the broader implementation of important initiatives.

LESSONS LEARNED

The chapters that follow record the most practical lessons that we gleaned from the Trustee Demonstration Project, especially about the dynamics and mechanics of effective governance. We also learned some larger, yet elementary, lessons about board development that boards of trustees and senior management would do well to grasp from the outset. These lessons, briefly stated here, are amplified throughout the book.

Lesson 1

Board development cannot be imposed on either trustees or an institution's president. For improvements to occur, both parties must be committed participants. The CEO and a substantial fraction of the trustees must recognize the importance of effective governance, acknowledge that the board could be more proficient, and earnestly commit themselves to the goal.

Lesson 2

Board development and the "real work" of the board are a false dichotomy. Board development must be *embedded* in the important issues, substantive agendas, and normal activities of the board. Trustees cannot be asked or expected to do the institution's business and then do board development. To be successful, board development must satisfy the instrumental expectations of trustees. In other words, the process must create real advantages that enable the board to work better and to produce results that redound to the institution's benefit.

Lesson 3

It is easier to change a board's behavior than a board's attitude or a trustee's personality. New routines, structures, or procedures are easier to effect and to institutionalize and are more likely than exhortation to lead to new outlooks about governance. Changes in structures, information systems, channels of communication, or orientation programs, for example, enable trustees to act differently and, as a result, to think differently about trusteeship (Weick 1983).

Lesson 4

Relatively significant, positive impact on board behavior can result from small, simple changes in structure, process, and procedures. The best board development devices marry process and substance. For example, when a board sets goals or creates a set of critical performance indicators, the process builds cohesion and educates trustees and, at the same time, the exercise generates an important, substantive product.

Lesson 5

Like professional or institutional development, board development must be approached as an intensive, long-term process and not a quick fix. To sustain the process, there must be among the trustees vigilant, ardent, "product champions" for board development, as fervid as the advocates of financial equilibrium. The tides are powerful, relentless, and unforgiving. Relax for a moment too long and the currents will sweep the board (and the institution) out to sea.

NOTES

1. At seminars we teach, we often ask college presidents to identify the most important contributions a board chair can make to the president's effectiveness. Inevitably, the presidents' list includes, at or near the top, items such as "nurturance," "care and feeding," and "taking care of the president."

2. This same observation was made about corporate boards by Jay Lorsch in "Empowering the Board" (1995) and by John Pound in "The Promise of the Governed Corporation" (1995).

3. We were introduced to the idea of team learning through practice by Peter Senge (1990) in *The Fifth Discipline: The Art and Practice of the Learning Organization*.

4. For further information on definitions, classifications, and methodologies, see Holland, Chait, and Taylor 1989, 435–53; and Holland, Taylor, Chait, and Jackson 1996.

5. We recognize that these opportunities may be severely curtailed at public institutions where laws require that the board meet in public, or potentially problematic at private institutions where students and faculty serve as trustees.

CHAPTER

2

•••••••••

Initiating and Sustaining Board Development

F ew boards are invited, as those at the Trustee Demonstration Project sites were, to participate in a comprehensive program of board development, externally designed and funded. In the real world of governance, CEOs and trustees, interested in enhancing their board's performance, are often unsure how to raise the issue, let alone how to proceed. In this chapter, we discuss how the processes and habits of board improvement can be initiated and sustained.

Most boards do not have a deep-rooted tradition of self-improvement. Any conscious and continuous efforts to strengthen the quality of trusteeship represent a departure from past practice and, therefore, a potential threat to trustees comfortable with current routines and doubtful that the possible benefits of change will outweigh the potential risks. In this sense, trustees are no different from anyone else. "The four most common reasons people resist change . . . include a desire not to lose something of value, a misunderstanding of the change and its implications, a belief that the change does not make sense for the organization, and a low tolerance for change" (Kotter and Schlesinger 1979, 107).

To many trustees, board development, at first blush, has little apparent utility. That assessment derives from two basic assumptions most trustees make about the linkage between what the board does and how well the institution performs: (1) an institution's success constitutes *prima facie* evidence of effective board performance; and (2) an institution's success renders superfluous any need to improve the board's performance. By either logic, a successful institution exonerates the board. Similarly, the board of an imperiled institution usually blames the administration, the faculty, the vicissitudes of the economy and the market, or just plain bad luck for the problems. Only rarely do trustees consider seriously that the board may have contributed to the institution's failure or that the board may have the unutilized capacity to ameliorate the situation through some action other than the dismissal of the CEO.

Because so many trustees perceive the relationship between the board's behavior and the institution's performance as ambiguous at best, any attempt to launch a board development program poses a particularly difficult challenge. As long as a board sees no clear link between what it does and how the institution fares, focusing the board's attention on improving its performance may seem like a nearly hopeless task.[1] But it is not. There are moments of opportunity and levers for change.

"SCARE 'EM AND SAVE 'EM"

"For an organization to change . . . it first must be destabilized" (Schein 1993, 88). Participants must come to believe that the failure to change is more dangerous than the discomfort and apprehension associated with attempts to learn and incorporate new behaviors. Thus, the first step toward board development is to create a sense of anxiety that attracts the trustees' attention.

Anxiety, however, can also cause fear, paralysis, and inaction. To foster change, therefore, leaders of reform must create an atmosphere of "psychological safety" that reassures the participants that change is both desirable and feasible. In other words, the board must first be unsettled and then be supported in the search for a new equilibrium. As one veteran trustee stated colloquially, the task is to "scare 'em and save 'em."

A new college president lucidly and bluntly explained to the board that, at then-current rates of tuition increases, endowment spending, and admissions yields, the school would be out of business in five years. The level of anxiety in the room was palpable. But at the same meeting, the president also suggested steps that the college could take to avert a catastrophe. The presentation precipitated a retreat where the board discussed institutional strategy, redesigned the trustee committee structure, and developed the elements of a program to educate board members about the issues central to the college's future—all steps intended to enable trustees to offer more informed input and oversight. In short, the process raised anxieties *and* provided the psychological safety that was necessary for the board to proceed with confidence.

This example illustrates some of the properties of a "psychologically safe" environment that offset the effects of anxiety. First, the troublesome issues were raised candidly and comprehensively. A good deal of anxiety within a board arises from the impression that there are ill-defined problems of unclear dimensions that the trustees have not analyzed and assessed together. The mere act of broaching, describing, and discussing the problem can ease anxieties. In addition, the president enumerated some possible responses. A board's anxiety subsides when someone whom the trustees respect, whether the president, the board chair, or a committee, provides leadership. Finally, the discussion at the board meeting prompted a concentrated effort to strengthen the trustees' grasp of the problem and the options and to augment the board's capacity to contribute to the solution.

In tandem, anxiety and "psychological safety" enable a board to change for the better. The effective board identifies the challenges to the institution that induce anxieties in its trustees and then creates a safe environment for them to confront and resolve these problems. Thus, the board institutionalizes an important habit or cycle: recognize problems, then change in response.

Today, many boards are sufficiently "scared" about their institution's future to urge or require that administration, professional staff, and faculty restructure, reengineer, and reinvent the institution in the spirit of continuous quality improvement. The trustees should expect no less of the board. Yet, such *internal* changes do not come naturally to many boards. As one chair explained, trustees are "uncomfortable with questions like 'How are we doing?' and 'How should we improve?' It's tough to get a group like this to be self-conscious. They're classic CEO types. They can tell stories about how their organizations are flatter, or how they're implementing employee empowerment and team building, but that's not how *they* got to where *they* are." Moreover, most trustees will not attend diligently to the board's performance without some assurance that the practical value of board development will warrant the efforts (and anxieties) that the change requires. This is precisely the argument that boards advance to administrative and professional staff and faculty opposed to institutional restructuring: the gain will justify the pain.

THE POWER OF INSTRUMENTALITY

Because trustees are, above all else, instrumental, board development must be perceived as a means to pursue discernable, desirable, institutionally related payoffs. Very simply, trustees care far more about how well the *institution* performs than how well the *board* performs.

Trustees express an almost universal aversion to noninstrumental board development—activities that may smooth the process or create goodwill but yield no other practical, tangible results. Many trustees worry that board development will amount to little more than "a lot of talky-talk with no action," or "a hot-tub exercise." These fears (or preconceived notions) largely account for the initial reservations among some trustees about the demonstration project:

A large portion of the board may have been initially skeptical because they perceived trustee development as navel gazing that would take time away from efforts to attend to the really important problems the college faced.

Those infrastructures set up on the side that are intended to improve board performance don't do it because they don't relate to reality, to what the board is really worried about.

For board development to be effective, you have to relate the soft stuff to the hard stuff.

The "message" from participants in the demonstration project was unambiguous: If board development can improve the board's ability to add value to the institution, then trustees will embrace the process and make the effort. Otherwise, more urgent matters—even the opportunity to adjourn early—will always take precedence.

POINTS OF ENTRY

There are occurrences in an institution's life that encourage a board to rethink the way it operates. Trustees and CEOs eager to start a board development effort should take advantage of these events as natural moments to initiate the process. Opportunities to plant the seeds of change include[2]

- the departure of the president
- changes in the board's leadership
- decisions involving competing priorities or forced choices, such as conflicts between mission and markets
- significant financial pressures or the need to launch a capital campaign
- dissatisfaction among key constituents, such as administrators, staff, faculty, students, donors, or alumni
- a violation of ethics within the board or the staff
- issues of board composition, membership, or retention, including the sense that the board lacks the right combination of skills or backgrounds
- fundamental questions raised by newcomers not familiar with the board's operating norms: "Why do we do this? Why don't we try that?"
- loss of a key source of revenue or changes in the priorities of a key resource provider such as federal or state government

Highly visible moments of transition, stress, or even crisis within an institution or a board, however traumatic otherwise, are particularly propitious opportunities for CEOs and trustees to initiate and pursue a board development effort.

Such occasions underscore, often publicly, the gap between a board's performance and the institution's needs and impel the board to consider new ways to do business. In truth, the more obvious and immediate the crisis, the *less* leaders generally need do to demonstrate the necessity for change, though the process must still be managed adroitly. The controversy over the exhibition of Mapplethorpe photographs at the Corcoran Gallery of Art, the scandal over a corrupt football program at Southern Methodist University, the nightmare at the United Way of America (Smith 1995)—events such as these galvanize the board's attention and make the case for change more apparent and usually more persuasive.

Rest assured that a board or an institution need not be cast into disrepute or crisis to capture the trustees' attention. The orderly transition to a new CEO offers the most obvious example. One college trustee noted, "I think that with a new president we will have to work a little harder, take a little more responsibility ourselves as trustees, rather than just following the president's lead. We'll have to think harder about what we're trying to accomplish." The chair of another board proposed that, prior to the search for a new president for the institution, the trustees consider where the institution had been and was headed. The discussion was intended to serve as a basis to establish the criteria for the search. More important, trustees raised and discussed questions about the board itself:

- How has this board helped lead the institution to where we are now?
- How did we contribute to the successes and failures of the outgoing president?
- What lessons should we draw from these experiences?
- What specifically should we do differently to work better with the new president?

In this instance, the fact that the trustees viewed themselves as a critical factor in the president's performance provided a rationale to address and improve the board's own effectiveness. The former president of another college offered a similar assessment: "Quite frankly, if your board can make itself good, you can get a better president than the institution would normally deserve to get. There may be a more tasteful way to say this, but a good board is a way to trade up in the presidential pool."

A prudent board that normally functions adequately can seize upon other, less tumultuous, occasions to change the way it operates. At a college, an unexpected enrollment shortfall, the decision of a competitor to cut tuition, complaints from restive new trustees, or loss of support from a sponsor can unsettle a board just enough to make change seem more desirable, and less risky, than the status quo. However, in the absence of institutional crisis or some other conspicuous need for change, leaders must do correspondingly more to pry open the door to board development.

Leaders can utilize information, communication, and other devices discussed later in this chapter to alter a board's perspective over time and thereby make the case for governance reforms more convincing. A college president, trained as a physicist, likened one board to molecules of an ideal gas at the temperature of absolute zero: lifeless. "A board first has to warm up enough to begin moving at all," he said. "So you need some steps to wake them up and help them begin to see what a board is supposed to be doing. Introducing board development activities was analogous to adding heat to the gas, thereby causing the molecules to awake from their resting state and begin moving." In simpler terms, a trustee said, "You have to fertilize the deal before you start watering."

To summarize, the more dramatic the transformation or the more dire the predicament a board or institution faces, the *less* leaders will have to document the case for board development and implore trustees to participate. At the other end of the spectrum, when an institution appears to be on an even keel and the natural points of entry to board development are not accessible, leaders must use proportionately greater leverage to cultivate the commitment to change within the board.

THE ROLES OF LEADERS AND OTHER CHANGE AGENTS

One board chair remarked, "It's fantastically difficult for a board to improve. The key is the president and the chair." Indeed, trustees and CEOs alike repeatedly acknowledged the need for leadership that acts intentionally to improve board performance. The board's leaders must, one administrator insisted, chant "the constant mantra of board development."

Anyone can raise questions about the board's effectiveness, but normally only the board's leadership or an influential committee can pursue the matter. It is simply too easy to ignore a single vocal trustee or marginalize a small, cluster of "malcontents." Leaders can *legitimate* collective attention to board performance. Leaders can create the forums and activate the procedures for trustees to discuss the board's effectiveness and to discover whether concerns about the board's performance are widespread or limited. A chair explained:

> After several people had come to me with their concerns about our long committee reports, I concluded that we really ought to bring this up with others and see if they felt that way too. What we found was that many people were dissatisfied but hadn't said anything. Then several folks said the prior issue was that they hadn't been very clear about the specific charges or responsibilities of their committees. That gave us a better sense

of where we had to go to work: clarifying the tasks of each committee. It was the step of coming to some agreement that we all wanted to make some changes that enabled us to move ahead and think together about possible solutions.

For many boards, the trusteeship committee or board affairs committee plays the most pivotal role in board development. With a broader charge than the typical nominating committee, the trusteeship committee bears explicit responsibility for board development, education, and assessment, as well as the recruitment of new members. Just as the finance committee trains the board's eye on budgetary and fiscal matters, and the development committee advocates attention to fundraising, a trusteeship committee can foster and legitimate the board's interest in self-development. At one college campus where board development has taken hold, a trustee cited the importance of advocacy for the process by the trusteeship committee: "When we were first invited to participate in the Trustee Demonstration Project, the committee met with the full board and went over all the details and what was required of us. They were so strongly supportive that everyone went along even though, for some of them, their hearts weren't really in it at the time."

Even if the CEO or board chair inaugurates a board development program, the trusteeship committee should soon assume permanent responsibility for the endeavor; otherwise, the departure or distraction of just one person can derail the process. By contrast, the presence of a group of trustees with knowledge and commitment to the process will ensure, in all likelihood, that the effort outlasts any one individual. As a board chair observed, "The way we've gotten our board to continue to pay attention to its own performance is by having the trusteeship committee meet at every board meeting and talk about it."

When the board's leadership or the designated committee fails to recognize or confront the board's inadequacies, individual trustees may press for change, albeit from a rather disadvantaged position. The CEO, the board chair, and the trusteeship committee control the agenda and the flow of information to trustees relative to board effectiveness and thus have the power to block as well as advance attention to board performance. Nevertheless, individual board members can (and sometimes do) call attention to the board's deficiencies and to the need for board development. Some are prompted to act by aspirations for the institution: "Younger and more capable trustees saw the board drifting and wanted change. They began speaking up about the need for goals, for growth, for direct attention to the college's real needs. They joined with each other to insist on getting to work on these issues." Sadly, however, far more are motivated by a combination of boredom and exasperation. Statements by two college trustees illustrate the frustration that, if heeded, can lead to positive change:

Frankly, I have better things to do with my time than sit in board meetings and listen to reports. I just don't understand why this place needs a board if this is all we're going to do.

Jack [a fellow trustee] said later that he would have liked to have found some other approach than suddenly calling for the president's resignation at the retreat, but he had tried everything else he could and had been unsuccessful. He admits it was an act of total frustration over the board's inaction, especially the leaders. Months and months had gone by with the problems just growing worse and worse. The board was concerned but paralyzed.

If the board's leaders are responsive and integrate such concerns into the group's overall effort, positive changes may ensue. If, on the other hand, the board's leadership fails to respond earnestly, the concerns will not disappear. Instead, dissatisfaction will be forced into "back channels" that eventually breed discontent and low morale. In other words, leaders may be able to block board development in the short run, but over the long run this obstinacy will create a wider point of entry for trustees determined to upgrade the board's performance.

To summarize, board development must be championed by an individual or group perceived to have the legitimacy to act. The institution's CEO, the board chair, other officers, the executive committee, or the trusteeship committee are the most likely prospects. Individual complaints and sidebar conversations by a subset of trustees without an established platform or a license to lead can sometimes kindle an interest in the board's performance; however, unless the board's leadership converts these initiatives into legitimate issues and purposeful action, the probability of a sustained program of board improvement will be remote. For leaders disposed to act, there are numerous levers available.

INFORMATION AND COMMUNICATION

Schein (1993) asserts that organizational participants are unlikely to accept that current modes of operation are inadequate and ineffective without "intense communication," usually by the group's leaders, of "disconfirming data . . . any items of information that show the organization that some of its goals are not being met or that some of its processes are not accomplishing what they are supposed to" (ibid., 299). In the case of a board, this communication needs to be embedded in information about the institution in order to underscore the board's relationship to institutional success.

Many senior managers, particularly CEOs, seem to accept as one of the administration's primary roles vis-à-vis the board a duty to periodically assure the trustees that "all's well." The typical CEO's report to the board, whether written or oral, accentuates institutional accomplishments and opportunities, individual achievements, and various indicators of the organization's stability. Such data reflect positively on the president and probably curb forays by the board into the operational realm—both desirable outcomes from the CEO's perspective. And while the board may be cheered by such reports, the message that the college faces no real challenges and that the president has a steady hand on the rudder can leave a board smug and self-satisfied. Why would trustees want to enhance the board's capabilities when the institution has no serious flaws and faces no major challenges?

We do not mean to imply that executives should alarm trustees unduly or fabricate problems where none exist. Rather, institutional leaders should convey succinct, forthright, strategic information that places the college's strengths and weaknesses in sharp relief. At a board retreat, for example, the president and senior officers of Duke University outlined the opportunities *and* the significant vulnerabilities that the institution would face over the next decade. A university that has enjoyed such meteoric success could understandably be complacent. To the contrary, the board welcomed the executives' candor, grappled with the matters at hand, *and* considered at some length the implications these challenges held for the board's capacity to "govern strategically." The staff provided vital, not alarming, information to the board that would have stemmed any temptation (had there been one) to be self-satisfied.

The lesson here is that "intense communication" by institutional leaders about issues of consequence makes the need for change within the board more overt and more imperative. A genuine crisis or a presidential transition serves as its own reminder of the board's responsibility. When the institution's circumstances or the board's obligations are less obvious, intense communication can raise the ante.

CEOs can enhance the trustees' commitment to improved performance through the presentation of important issues for active consideration by the board. When the stakes seem high, trustees are more likely to question whether the board is equipped, organized, and educated to handle matters of real magnitude. When the issues are marginal or unimportant, trustees find the value of board development difficult to comprehend. After all, when the questions before the board are "no brainers," why would any trustee not feel equal to the task?

Comparative data are especially useful to increase trustees' awareness of the institution's relative performance, position, and condition. One trustee said, "You have to build benchmarking into the board. Otherwise how will trustees know how good the school is?" A senior administrator added, "The keys to improving the board's performance are the usual ones: good ideas, well presented and externally validated—by national publications, outside consultants, and the like. Trustees need some outside basis for comparison in order to understand how the university is doing."

As high achievers, most board members are intensely competitive and want to be affiliated with a board and an institution that excels. Board leaders can use the trustees' inclination toward competitiveness to encourage needed change. If the data indicate some vulnerability or slippage, chances are the board will want to reduce the institution's exposure or reverse a downward drift. The same data, frankly interpreted, will spur the board to become better because the information provides the board with a *reason* to become better. Likewise, data that reveal a positive momentum for which the board feels at least partly responsible will energize the board to reach the next plateau of excellence or the next tier of endowed wealth.

FRESH PERSPECTIVES

Groups with stable membership can become insular and self-satisfied. Without exposure to new points of view and a fresh perspective on the board's performance, many trustees become blind to either the desirability or possibility of change.

The expectations and experiences of new members can provide a powerful stimulus for change. New trustees often have different assumptions about governance and ask "naive" questions about the board's operations that encourage a critical reexamination of its beliefs and behaviors. One such dramatic revelation occurred when a brand new trustee innocently asked just after roll call, "What are the board's goals for this meeting?" The question stunned everyone and forced the board to acknowledge that there were no explicit aims; the tacit objective was to complete the laundry list of items on the agenda (and adjourn on time). Thereafter, the chair started each meeting with an overview of its purposes. A board chair and a trustee described the value of new blood on their boards:

> We had some new members who had served on other boards, and they started telling us about some ways those boards had dealt with a problem we were facing. That led to our asking how they had handled several other issues. As a result, we've imported some good ideas that just never occurred to us before.

> The board changed because of a change in composition. The impetus [for board development] came initially from a new member who had been cultivated by the president.

Such experiences have persuaded more and more boards to institute term limits. In a survey by the Association of Governing Boards of Universities and Colleges (AGB 1991), 57% of independent colleges and 29% of public colleges restricted the number of consecutive terms trustees could serve. (The median was three terms for independent institutions and two terms for public institutions.) While no formula can serve equally well the situations of all boards, the need to balance continuity and turnover suggests a "window of opportunity" every three years or so to reassess a trustee's contributions and the board's needs. After perhaps 9 or 12 years, there would be a mandatory rotation off the board for at least 1 year. A board chair explained:

> Before we established term limits, we already knew how everyone thought, which is one reason it is good that we instituted rotations. You can get stagnant, just because you have done things the same way for so long—not that we were archaic, but we needed new blood.

Even with term limits, the trustees' capacity for change can be constrained by provisions that restrict membership to a potentially homogeneous population; for example, on a college board, only alumni or only members of a particular denomination. A board chair said, "I think it is important in the near term to bring on some people who are committed to the college but who aren't alumni and can provide a very different perspective on higher education, or society, or whatever else." If, for some reason, the institution must confine eligibility to a certain pool of candidates, the board's insights can still be enriched by visiting committees, ad hoc task forces, study groups, and other nonboard bodies, and by the inclusion of some nontrustees on board committees where the board's bylaws permit. A veteran university trustee explained, "The Commission on the Future of the University was set up to be a fundraising gimmick but I took it seriously. I used it as a device to shake the place up." Another trustee added, "The Commission brought 200 outsiders into the campus to give us new perspectives on ourselves."

Many trustees and CEOs believe that outside experts can also help induce change within a board. Like the ideas of new members and external constituents, the perspectives of outside experts can substantiate the need for change and delineate multiple paths to achieve the desired state. One trustee's best advice to other boards about how to improve was to "get some outside help for training, some tools and technical assistance to help you focus your time and attention, to offer you ideas and possibilities you might not have known about, some coaching in the use of them, and some ideas about how to get right to the big issues and not waste time on tangents."

Trustees caution, however, that outside help will not substitute for commitment by the board and president. As two board chairs observed:

You can't just come up with a list of things that make a board better and then just tell people how to do it.

Every board has a personality. No amount of outside coercion will make them do anything. You need leadership within the board, but outside help is very useful for providing new perspectives and ideas. You just can't *change* a board from the outside.

On the inside, however, boards and staff can use materials, techniques, and devices developed by researchers or trustee organizations. The former president of a college that participated in the Trustee Demonstration Project and later introduced board development at another institution reported, "I just tore off the pages of what I learned and brought it with me when I moved. It is absolutely easily replicable. We've added educational components, instituted a trustee orientation program, written a board handbook, and started a trusteeship committee."

HOW DO WE KNOW HOW WELL WE ARE DOING AS A BOARD?

Once trustees decide that the board's effectiveness can and should be improved, questions often arise about whether and how to evaluate the board's progress. Trustees are sometimes reluctant to undertake a methodical evaluation of the board's performance. Among the arguments commonly advanced against such assessments are: (1) the criteria, standards, and benchmarks are vague; (2) evaluations are inappropriate for volunteers; and (3) there are no empirically valid evaluation techniques.

Although each of these contentions has some merit, none should deter a board. The paramount goals of board evaluations are not precise comparisons, individual appraisals, and scientific accuracy. Rather, assessment offers a practical means—an "excuse" or catalyst—to initiate and sustain attention to board performance, to stimulate self-reflection, and to track changes over time. Assessment spotlights the board's performance, just as a review of the annual audit rivets trustees' attention to financial performance. Without regular evaluations of the board's effectiveness, the issue can easily disappear from the trustees' radar screen.

Trustees often mentioned the importance of evaluation as a crucial first step toward improved performance. Three trustees of different colleges offered remarkably similar advice: "Initially, you should assess the board's current skills, talents, concerns, and needs, and then use that information to plan how to approach learning." "I would tell them to start by evaluating the present performance of the board." "Start with an assessment of your board's strengths and weaknesses."

Especially at the onset of board development, the exact tools and tech-niques a board uses are less important than establishing the precedent and custom of constructive self-reflection. The goal, stated one board member, is to provide "fairly regular opportunities for trustees to step up and say, 'There might be a better way for our committee to do this,' or 'We have some suggestions and questions, and here they are.'"

Assessment can take many forms; each method has advantages and drawbacks. The approaches described below, arrayed from least to most comprehensive, all serve a developmental purpose: to focus the trustees' attention on board effectiveness and to spur discussions about improved performance.

Fast Feedback

Some professors now ask students, after each class, to submit comments anonymously on index cards about the quality and value of that session. This so-called "fast feedback" has proven to be very useful to both parties.

The approach can easily be transferred from the classroom to the board-room. At the end of each board or committee meeting, the chair can invite written (or oral) comments about the session. In most cases, the chair shares the responses with the CEO or the appropriate staff liaison. Some boards use a standard form (see Exhibit 2.1), while others vary the form to seek reactions to the special features of a particular meeting (see Exhibit 2.2) One chair asks trustees to "just tell us what you thought of the meeting" on a 3-by-5 index card distributed and collected on the spot. This procedure "has been very helpful, and we know what we're doing right as well as what we could do better."

Meeting Evaluation Form I				
	Not Very Important			Very Important
The issues covered were	1	2	3	4	5
	Unfocused			Focused
The discussion was	1	2	3	4	5
	Confusing			Informative
The materials provided were	1	2	3	4	5
	Less than Adequate		More than Was Needed	
	1	2	3	4	5
	Limited Participation		Full Participation	
The meeting structure allowed	1	2	3	4	5

EXHIBIT 2.1

Meeting Evaluation Form II

A. **General** (Check all that apply)
   1. Written materials sent in advance of the meeting were
      _____ Too extensive
      _____ Too summary
      _____ Dealt with the right issues
      _____ Did not give sufficient attention to the issue of
      _____ or _____
      The materials could be improved by _____

   2. Logistics/arrangements/hospitality
      Please jot down any areas (ranging from parking to lodging, dining to _____
      scheduling) that might be improved _____

B. **On-campus sessions**
   One of the recommendations we have heard is that we need to reduce the
   amount of time devoted to reporting and allow additional time for discussion.
   Some committees, of course, can accomplish this interaction more readily
   than others. Please indicate if less reporting is needed, or add other
   suggestions.
   Student Affairs: _____
   Educational Affairs: _____
   President's Breakfast: _____
   Enrollment Committee: _____
   Finance Committee: _____
   Lunch with English Department: _____
   Buildings and Grounds Committee: _____
   Membership Committee: _____
   Development Committee: _____
   Investment Committee: _____
   Dinner at the President's House: _____
   Executive Sessions: _____
   Breakout Brainstorming Sessions: _____
   Board Meeting: _____

C. **Suggestions for future meetings**
   A plenary session on the college's financing (and fund accounting) has been
   suggested. What other topics would you like to see reviewed in a plenary
   session? _____

   In the last two meetings, we visited the science faculty and heard from the
   English faculty. Are there particular parts of the education program or groups
   of faculty you recommend for inclusion in an upcoming board meeting? _____

   Other comments and suggestions: _____

D. **Fall meeting**
   When we changed the format last fall for the October meeting to Friday–
   Saturday instead of Thursday–Friday, attendance fell. For next year, would
   you prefer:
   Thursday–Friday, October 21–22 _____
   Friday–Saturday, October 22–23 _____

E. **Committee assignments**
   List other/different committee assignments you would prefer for next
   year _____

EXHIBIT 2.2

A board can also provide feedback in an executive session, where the trustees meet privately, normally with the institution's CEO in attendance. A chair explained, "At the end of each meeting, we ask our members how it went and if there are ways we could do it better." Questions this board discusses include:

- How well did we do our work at this meeting?
- Did we get the right information early enough to prepare for the meeting?
- Did we use our time well?
- Did we deal with important issues?
- Are we doing what we should to support the president and the staff?
- Are there other concerns or questions we should discuss?

The benefits of fast feedback (and other evaluation techniques) extend well beyond the information produced about the board's performance. In addition to improving meetings, a trustee noted, fast feedback "has made attention to the board's performance a conscious focus and a legitimate issue for board attention." That is, the very act of soliciting feedback legitimated board performance as a matter for consideration.

As more than one chair has observed, the credibility of the process hinges on immediate and tangible results. Trustees must be able to see changes that are directly responsive to their expressed concerns. A chair explained, "We have evaluations after every meeting, and we follow through on people's suggestions and follow up with those people whose suggestions we don't accept, to explain why."

Self-Assessment Instruments

Almost as easy to use as fast feedback, self-assessment instruments—typically, questionnaires—are probably the most common approach trustees use to evaluate the board's performance. Groups such as AGB, the National Center for Nonprofit Boards (NCNB), and the National Association of Independent Schools (NAIS) have developed self-assessment instruments in which trustees rate substantive aspects of board performance. The AGB *Self-Study Criteria* (1986), with separate versions for various types of public and private institutions, addresses the board's performance with respect to

- mission and policy
- institutional planning
- financial support and management
- physical facilities
- board membership and organization

- assessment and support of the chief executive
- board-staff relations
- relationship with external constituencies

Self-assessment offers the virtues of simplicity, economy, and efficiency. The approach also presents little risk, since board members complete the forms anonymously, and conclusions about the board's performance are simply the sum of trustees' opinions, rather than an external judgment. Moreover, use of the AGB, NCNB, and NAIS instruments, all organized around basic governance responsibilities, reinforces among board members a shared view of trusteeship.

On the downside, self-assessments are notoriously unreliable as a gauge of a board's actual (as opposed to perceived) performance (Holland 1991). For reasons that range from ego protection to the lack of any sound basis for comparison, most trustees cannot judge their own board's performance accurately. In fact, an analysis of results from 61 boards that had completed the AGB *Self-Study Criteria* revealed no significant differences among the boards' self-perceptions. Virtually every one concluded that its performance, overall and in each area of board responsibility, was well above average (Chait and Taylor 1987).

Clearly, self-assessment can leave trustees unjustifiably self-content. This risk can be mitigated, however, when the results are reviewed at a board retreat or some other extended discussion moderated by an adept facilitator, experienced enough to place the data in a broader, comparative context and competent enough to raise ticklish issues that the board might otherwise sidestep.

A third self-assessment instrument (Exhibit 2.6, at the end of the chapter), based on the six dimensions of board effectiveness summarized in Chapter 1, emerged directly from the research that we conducted. As with other self-study instruments, each trustee completes the form anonymously. However, the responses on the *Board Self-Assessment Questionnaire* cannot be tallied locally; they must be tabulated by the survey's designers. The results include scores on each of the six competencies, as well as comparative data from other nonprofit boards that have used the instrument.

The *Board Self-Assessment Questionnaire* offers the advantage of a behavioral focus. Unlike the AGB, NCNB, or NAIS surveys, the questionnaire measures the board's performance on specific behaviors associated with effective trusteeship, pinpoints areas that a board needs to strengthen, and offers various suggestions to remedy areas of relative weakness. Thus, the questionnaire provides more guidance for the board that wishes to move from self-evaluation to self-improvement.

Constituent Feedback

Unlike other groups and individuals within a nonprofit institution, a governing board has no built-in sources of evaluation. Professional staff members assess the performance of their subordinates or students, the chief administrator assesses senior officers, coworkers and colleagues provide feedback to one another, and those who use the institution's services provide feedback to the staff. But who has been charged to assess the board? If the trustees expect an institution's staff or faculty and administrators to seek and use feedback, then should the board not exhibit the same behavior? It is not as if constituents lack opinions about the board's performance; rather, they have no official channels to communicate those opinions to the trustees. To do so, especially outside established avenues or without invitation, usually carries exceptionally high risk. In one unusual case, a college president related, "I write an annual report to the executive committee about my own performance. They've established a requirement that I also tell the board how well I think *they're* doing." Without such a mandate, few CEOs—or other stakeholders—are likely to volunteer an appraisal of the board.

Trustees typically believe, with some justification, that no one beyond the institution's CEO and senior staff has the requisite knowledge to offer an informed assessment of the board's performance. And, indeed, large-scale surveys of constituents are less valuable than targeted discussions, since survey respondents are probably not sufficiently cognizant of the board's role and performance. In the few institutions where boards do seek constituency feedback, virtually all of the questions concern institutional rather than board performance. The board of one college, for example, annually convenes civic leaders to discuss the quality of the college's graduates. At best, this board might draw some indirect inferences from these conversations about its effectiveness.

At the very least, a board should seek performance feedback from the CEO and senior staff to board committees. Moreover, a board can benefit from periodic conversations with leaders of professional staff, administrator, student, alumni, and other groups about what the board's priorities should be. In an exemplary case, the trustees of a prominent research university retained outside experts to collect feedback on the board's performance. The board concluded that, because the institution required that all programs and offices be assessed every five years, the board should not and could not be exempt from a comparable review. A board chair and a president emeritus from similar institutions were invited to conduct informal conversations with trustees, senior staff, and select community, faculty, and student leaders. For a nominal fee (which both later donated to the university), the consultants provided concise written and oral reports to the board, which precipitated certain changes in the board's structure and operations.

Governance Audit

To concentrate intensively on board performance, a few boards have engaged in a governance audit, a comprehensive review by expert outsiders. Typically, the external consultants interview the chair, a cross section of board members, the institution's president, senior staff, and sometimes others acquainted with the board's work. The consultants also observe board and committee meetings, and they review bylaws, committee structures, and trustee information packets. To elicit the views of all board members, the consultants may also administer a standard self-assessment survey. Ordinarily, the review culminates with a written and oral report to the trustees that includes constituent perceptions of the board's performance, the board's self-assessment, and the consultants' professional evaluation and recommendations. The audit frequently serves as a precursor to a retreat on improving the board's performance.

Due to the comprehensive nature of the process, reinforced by a follow-up action plan, significant improvements can occur over a relatively short period of time, usually between 6 and 18 months. Then, every five years or so, another governance audit can punctuate the less extensive evaluations done at meetings, through annual surveys, or at occasional retreats.

A governance audit has several advantages. Interviews allow more nuanced responses than surveys, and conversations conducted by outside experts are likely to elicit more candid comments. Professional consultants can also place the information gathered into a larger comparative context. Like a good anthropologist, the governance auditor will make the familiar strange and the strange familiar. On the other hand, precisely because the experts are external, the board can repudiate conclusions or shelve recommendations that, for whatever reason, the trustees or the CEO deem unpleasant or unacceptable. Lastly, while the process saves board and staff time, the cost of a governance audit can reach $30,000 or more.

Evaluation of Individual Trustees

Assessments of the board's effectiveness lead almost inevitably to questions about whether, why, and how to evaluate the performance of individual trustees. Chapter 3 discusses the difficulties intrinsic to the evaluation of individual board members. As that chapter suggests, a more useful tactic may be to emphasize trustee *development* and not trustee *assessment*. The former has a constructive, developmental purpose—to cultivate and engage trustee talent—whereas the latter has a more summative, judgmental flavor.

A focus on development rather than evaluation holds more promise as a way to change trustee behavior. The section on "Using Trustee Talent and Expertise" in Chapter 3 mentions several techniques to nurture a trustee's potential, such as a process for board members to set specific personal goals or to accept particular assignments. These approaches educate trustees about strategic priorities, fortify commitments to work on the college's behalf, and develop the practice of self-reflection on the part of individual trustees—all essential ingredients to board development.

Some boards do invite trustees to complete the self-appraisal section of the AGB, NCNB, or NAIS self-study surveys (see "Self-Assessment Instruments," above). On those forms, trustees rate their own performance in areas such as knowledge of trusteeship and the institution, participation in board and committee meetings, and commitment to fundraising and advocacy. The anonymous responses can be aggregated to provide a comprehensive self-portrait of the board, or the instrument can be completed and considered privately by each board member. Either way, the process encourages self-analysis and averts the resentment and divisiveness that can result from individual "report cards" based on peer judgments.

While formal assessments of individual trustees have limited value and a substantial downside, less formal approaches can be constructive. These include informal discussions by the trusteeship committee about how to motivate apathetic trustees, private conversations between the chair and trustees who are not performing well, new assignments to rejuvenate dormant members, and, as a last resort, rotation of nonperformers off the board.

BOARD RETREATS

The Value of Retreats

Because boards are so instrumental, trustees are often skeptical at the outset about the value of retreats. Many wince at the mere suggestion of such a day-long, off-site venture. The skeptics, quite understandably, fear that the retreat will be all talk and no action, an exercise to *feel* better, not *do* better. Some have attended "touchy-feely" retreats in the past or have worked hard at substantive retreats only to see the organization quickly revert to business as usual. Three trustees described the problem in similar terms:

> The three R's of retreats are Rhetoric, Reflection, and Recreation. There's no fourth R for Results.

> We had many on the board who were very dubious and thought the retreat would be a touchy-feely kind of thing. But because we had a good experience, it provided a good trajectory for the whole board development effort.

> It can't be a touchy-feely retreat. It has to be based on some critical issue, a discussion with true meaning.

Despite the apprehensions of some, veteran trustees and seasoned presidents almost always cite retreats as the single most powerful lever to direct attention to board effectiveness and to devise the means to strengthen board performance. Two presidents remarked:

> Adding an annual retreat made more difference than anything else we've done to improve the board.

> The number one change we've made has been the commitment to begin each year with a retreat. This has allowed the trustees to be more relaxed and spontaneous with more time for discussion. This sets the tone for the entire year.

Trustees expressed similar sentiments:

> Retreats build ownership. They are a great kickoff and starting point.

> The retreat helped us to begin to think about ourselves, to be reflective about our own performance, and to broaden our understanding of the board and its functions.

Trustees and CEOs cited many specific outcomes from productive retreats such as a firmer grasp of the institution's strategic challenges and priorities, a deeper appreciation of complex issues such as technology and funding, better use of the board's time, a reconfigured committee structure, a revamped orientation program, and new avenues for two-way communication with key constituencies.

As reported by trustees and chief executives, the general features that make retreats worthwhile include a clear purpose, a license to brainstorm, and the time to think without the imperative to act. More specific elements include: an agenda limited to a few high stakes issues; a task-oriented, problem-solving format; small work groups as well as plenary sessions; informality; and enough unscheduled time to foster camaraderie.

Of paramount importance, however, successful retreats are constructed on a cornerstone of trustee commitment to the process. How can the board's leaders and the institution's president build broad enthusiasm and ownership for a retreat?

Building Trustee Commitment to a Retreat

Develop a Shared Purpose

A chair, a CEO, a trusteeship committee, or some other influential group of trustees can test and bolster a board's commitment to a proposed retreat by leading a plenary discussion of the general purposes of the retreat. Why should the board have a retreat at this time? What would trustees like to see happen as a result? Do we want to focus exclusively on governance issues, such as roles and responsibilities, board composition, trustee education, and constituent relations, or do we want to consider institutional strategy and the board's role with respect to strategic issues?

Given the practical bent of most boards, a large majority, of course, favor a retreat that combines a general discussion of strategic institutional priorities with work sessions on how to equip and position a board to deal with these matters. While retreats can serve various specific purposes, the board's discussion typically produces some combination of the following purposes:

- to strengthen board performance through a review of governance processes and the board's role
- to assess the board's contributions to the organization and to identify ways the board can add greater value
- to establish priorities for the board and to develop an action plan to achieve those goals
- to enhance collegiality and working relationships among board members and between board and staff
- to determine the next steps in board development and the implementation of action plans

Ensure Attendance

The board must decide whether any of the institution's staff, beyond the president, will participate in the retreat. In general, this decision depends on the purposes of the retreat. If the agenda deals chiefly or exclusively with board issues, then attendance should probably be restricted to trustees and the chief executive (along with an aide to take notes and manage logistics). Alternatively, the board may decide that staff should be present, primarily as observers, in order to understand better the board's concerns and intentions, and the role staff should play to be most helpful. If the retreat centers on institutional issues, staff could attend to serve as resource people for all or part of the event. If the board decides to exclude senior administrators altogether, then the president and the chair should meet with them, shortly after the event, to summarize the overall discussion and to highlight the retreat's implications and the board's expectations for staff.

Some boards include trustee spouses at retreats, especially at meals and social events. In general, retreats—especially those of short duration—are more productive if spouses do not attend. At lengthier retreats, with ample time available for recreation and social events, the inclusion of spouses may be more practical.

To solidify commitment to the retreat, the board should adopt a formal resolution that pledges a good faith effort on the part of all trustees to attend and to participate.

Establish a Planning Committee

Once the board, as a whole, has established the purposes of the retreat, determined the "guest list," and formally resolved to proceed, the trustees should designate an ad hoc or standing committee to plan the details and manage the follow-up process. Because a retreat committee is crucial to build ownership of the process beyond the president and chair, its membership should be broadly representative of the board in terms of composition and points of view.

The five- to seven-member planning committee, including the president and chair, designs (with or without an external facilitator) the format and content of the event. At the retreat, committee members serve as advocates and monitors of the process and as navigators for the inevitable mid-course corrections in the agenda. Subsequent to the retreat, the planning committee constitutes a logical choice to oversee the initial stages of follow-up.

Appoint a Facilitator

The retreat planning committee should discuss whether or not to use an outside facilitator.[3] If the committee decides to do so, the facilitator should be asked to meet at least once with the committee prior to the retreat, for several hours. The facilitator should inquire about the purposes of the retreat; the desired outcomes; and the board's history, culture, and sensitivities. The facilitator should then draft, and redraft as necessary, a retreat plan consistent with the board's needs and the organization's culture.

At the retreat, a skillful facilitator moderates discussions, encourages participation, raises provocative questions, presses the board to surface and address conflicts, suggests various tactics to strengthen the board's performance, assists trustees to reach consensus, and helps identify action steps for post-retreat follow-up. As trustees attest, an outside facilitator provides important benefits: "It's good to have someone hold a mirror up to you, to show you how you look to others." "It's hard to be honest without an outsider who cares being there to keep you honest."

Elicit Trustees' Opinions

The facilitator may ask or be asked to interview a broader range of trustees to learn more about the board's views and to build credibility for the retreat process, particularly if some members still doubt its value or if significant differences exist among trustees about the board's role or the institution's course.

In addition to interviews—or instead of them—the retreat committee may decide to administer one of the self-assessment instruments described earlier. Survey data may reveal issues that trustees would like to discuss at the retreat, and may provide other helpful information about board members' anxieties or aspirations. Moreover, just the act of asking board members for their opinions, whether through a survey or interviews, will help build a constituency of support for the retreat and for the action steps to follow.

Select the Right Time and Place

If possible, the retreat should extend over all or part of two days in an informal setting, away from the institution, or at least apart from the board's usual meeting place. The facility need not be an elegant hotel or resort; in fact, such sites can offer too many distractions. Corporate conference facilities can be ideal, as can church camps and other relatively primitive facilities whose very simplicity seems to enhance camaraderie.

The only real requirements, besides dining and sleeping facilities, are a meeting room large enough to accommodate the board at a U-shaped or hollow square table and break-out space sufficient to accommodate work groups. In order to lower interpersonal barriers and set a tone of informality and candor, participants should be encouraged to dress casually. While concern for arrangements and logistics may seem trivial, attention to such details produces an atmosphere that encourages trustees to think creatively and to interact dynamically.

Hone the Agenda

The retreat agenda should be substantive and reflective of the input board members provided to the planning committee. The issues on the table should be plainly worthy of the trustees' commitment of additional time and energy. The design should foster inclusiveness, forthrightness, and an action orientation, "with a minimum of long-winded speeches by anyone," as one trustee cautioned. "What worked at our retreat was that we opened with a group discussion and a brainstorming session about interesting issues. It really got people moving and thinking."

While every retreat differs in the details, a prototype can be sketched, such as the sample agenda in Exhibit 2.3. Many begin with comments by the president and/or the board chair that reiterate the central purposes of the event and place the retreat in a broader institutional or governance context. The facilitator might then describe the flow and format of the retreat, the tasks to be accomplished, and the follow-up procedures, so that trustees are assured at the very outset of the action-oriented nature of the event. If the retreat focuses on institutional strategy, the president might describe the key challenges and opportunities the institution faces.

Sample Board Retreat Agenda

FRIDAY

Noon	**Lunch Available**
1:00 p.m.	**Welcome and Introductions by the Chair**
1:15	**The President's Perspective**

The president will highlight key issues of policy and strategy that are likely to come before the board for discussion and/or decision in the next 12–24 months. In so doing, the president will foreshadow the early thinking and policy options arising from the strategic planning process on campus.

2:00   General Discussion

Do any of the issues outlined by the president require clarification or elaboration? Are these indeed important issues for the college? Are there any other crucial questions that the board will have to help define and resolve in the next year or two? By the conclusion of these two segments of the retreat, there should be a general consensus among trustees about the questions and decisions that will demand the board's attention for the foreseeable future.

2:45   Break

3:00   Small Working Groups, Session #1

Trustees will be divided into working groups of approximately 7–8 persons to develop some initial reactions to the emergent strategic plan. In this way, trustees can provide feedback to the strategic planning committee and help shape the very nature and content of the plan as it is further refined. Among the questions each working group should consider are:

• What are the most attractive elements of the plan?

• What are your most significant concerns or reservations?

• What's the best advice that you can offer to those responsible for drafting the plan?

4:15   Report Back #1

Each group will have up to 10 minutes to report its major conclusions and key points. A general discussion will follow with the goal of identifying common themes and best ideas.

5:30   Recess

6:30   Dinner

EXHIBIT 2.3

continued

SATURDAY

7:00 a.m.	**Breakfast available**
8:00	**Adding Value As a Board**

The retreat facilitator will describe some of the best practices of effective governing boards as regards focusing on strategic issues, ensuring consequential board meetings, having meaningful information, and functioning as a cohesive group.

9:15   **Small Working Groups, Session #2**

Again working in small groups, trustees will be asked to consider how the board can do business better in light of institutional strategy and in light of best practices elsewhere. Among the questions to be considered are:

- What are the three most useful, practical steps we could take within the next six months to be a more effective, more strategically focused board?
- What more fundamental changes, if any, should we consider over the next year or so, for example, as regards committee structure or the format of board and committee meetings?

10:15   **Break**

10:30   **Report Back #2**

Each group will have up to 10 minutes to report its best thinking and most attractive proposals. A general discussion will follow to seek consensus and to outline a concrete action plan that will improve the way the board does business.

11:15   **Plenary Discussion**

In this session, we will develop substantive meeting plans for the board for the next 12 months. What topics and themes should be emphasized? Are there any "knowledge gaps" within the board—areas where we are not well-informed—that need to be closed? The goal is to design a series of board meetings for the year ahead that will be exciting to attend and that will enable the board to add still greater value to the college.

Noon   **Summary and Evaluation**

All trustees will have a minute to express their hopes and concerns about governing the college. We will close with comments from the president and the chair of the board about next steps and follow-up after the retreat.

12:45 p.m. **Adjournment**

EXHIBIT 2.3 (continued)

Trustees should spend much of the retreat in *working groups* of six to eight people. Each group should be given specific assignments, usually to be completed in 90 minutes to two hours, that are obviously related to the goals that the board set for the retreat. In most instances, each group has a different task, although sometimes when one issue is dominant (e.g., a mismatch between mission and market, or confusion about the board's basic role), all work groups might tackle the same assignment.

In any event, the assignment should always be explicitly linked to post-retreat action. Otherwise, the retreat will promote pleasant conversations that yield no concrete plans to improve the board's performance. To illustrate, a group could have an animated discussion about the board's strengths and weaknesses, but it will lead nowhere unless the group has been directed, for example, to list three specific actions that will link the board's agenda to institutional priorities, or that will align the structure and work of the board's committees with the college's strategic goals, or that outlines a step-by-step procedure to nominate and appoint the board's officers. Other assignments might be: to devise an orientation program for new board members, or to devise a "dashboard" (see Chapter 4) to monitor the effectiveness of the college or the board. Each group should be pressed, as well, to answer the question, "Who needs to do what, and by when?"

The value of small work groups cannot be overstated. This structure multiplies the number of tasks that can be accomplished, increases the total air time available, engenders participation (especially by trustees hesitant to speak in large groups), provides a safe environment to think creatively or even radically, and better acquaints trustees with one another.

The planning committee should designate for each work group one trustee to guide the discussion and encourage widespread participation, and another to record and later report the group's conclusions at the plenary session that follows the group discussion. Exhibit 2.4 provides a fuller description of these roles.

At the plenary sessions, the facilitator should moderate the discussion of group reports, help the board identify common themes, highlight the most attractive ideas, and outline the next steps. For example, if a small group designs an orientation program, the plenary discussion might concern whether the content and format of the proposed program are appropriate and sufficient and where responsibility for follow-up should reside.

Toward the end of the retreat, time should be reserved to summarize and prioritize the board's major conclusions. If the agenda and the small-group assignments have been designed properly and the discussion managed skillfully, areas of consensus should be obvious, and the delineation of relative priorities should be straightforward. To reinforce consensus, each participant can be asked to share briefly a final comment, concern, or hope. This act reinforces the principle of equal participation and involvement and provides closure to the event. Lastly, the chair and president should outline the steps that will be taken to implement the ideas generated at the retreat.

Guidelines for Conveners and Reporters

During the course of the retreat, participants will be divided on occasion into small work groups. This format should make it easier for everyone to participate in a lively conversation. In all instances, each work group will be expected to produce a written summary of its deliberations. Newsprint, markers, and masking tape will be provided to each group for this purpose. In addition, each group will be expected to provide a pithy oral report to the large group, highlighting significant conclusions and recommendations. The work groups and their written and oral reports are essential to a successful and productive retreat. Each group will have a convener and a reporter to help facilitate its work.

The Convener should:
- Encourage the group to assemble quickly and get down to work.
- Review briefly the assignment.
- Guide the discussion, making sure that each person has a chance to participate fully, if necessary inviting quieter individuals to share their thinking with the group.
- Monitor available time to ensure that all major issues are addressed.
- Stimulate discussion through questions or by asking members of the group to converse with each other, rather than just proceeding from one comment to another without any attempt to connect them.
- Help the group reach consensus rather than resort to voting.
- Leave some time for group members to summarize and synthesize the major points of the discussion.

The Reporter will be responsible for capturing on newsprint the essence of the group's discussion and then communicating the results to the board as a whole.

The Reporter should:
- Record the main points of the discussion.
- Check with the group as he/she goes along to make sure that the statement is an accurate reflection of what was intended.
- Help look for common themes as well as areas of disagreement.
- Post each page on the wall as the discussion proceeds so that everyone has a visual record of the discussion.
- Take some time toward the end of the period to record on newsprint the major points or "headlines" the group would like to communicate at the plenary session.
- Print legibly and large enough that the newsprint can be read by all participants in the main meeting room.

EXHIBIT 2.4

Ensure Follow-up

Most retreats generate a great deal of positive momentum that, regrettably, evaporates quickly unless follow-up activities occur swiftly and visibly. Within a day or two after the retreat, the institution's president, board chair, or members of the retreat planning committee should telephone, individually or by conference call, all absent trustees to describe the event, the outcomes, and the next steps, and to respond to any questions or concerns the trustees may raise. The board might also request that a brief report on the retreat be distributed to faculty, staff, or other stakeholders in order to dispel any false rumors about the retreat and to convey the board's seriousness of purpose.

Excerpts from a Post-retreat Action Plan		
Action	**Responsibility**	**Timeline**
Establish ongoing programs and curriculum for board education.	Board Affairs Committee	First program to be given at fall board meeting. First year curriculum to be approved by board at fall board meeting.
Establish a process to plan for transition and development of board and presidential leadership.	Executive Committee and Board Affairs Committee	Joint meeting to be held in July. Progress report to board in fall.
Establish a communication plan to keep board members informed of campus issues.	President and Advancement Committee	Meet within the month to develop plan. Begin enhanced communication immediately after meeting. Describe plan at fall meeting.
Implement President's Hour at each meeting.	President	Fall board meeting.
Create a dashboard with up to 10 gauges to reflect institutional performance.	Special "Dashboard Task Force" (4 trustees, 4 administrators)	Meet over the summer. Send draft to all trustees and senior staff. Discuss and adopt at fall meeting.
Create a trustee manual of policies, procedures, and practices.	Subcommittee of Board Affairs Committee, plus 2 or 3 administrators	Meet as needed to complete draft manual by spring board meeting. Update board meetings in the interim.

EXHIBIT 2.5

As soon after the retreat as possible—a few weeks at most—the retreat committee, preferably with the facilitator, should draft a plan to pursue priority actions identified at the retreat. The committee should have a detailed written record of the retreat's deliberations, usually prepared by the staff secretary to the board, that captures the essence of the work groups and the major conclusions from the plenary sessions.

The retreat committee should review the entire list of proposals and cull the ideas that enjoyed the broadest support or exhibit the greatest potential. Because the board will want to see immediate results from the retreat, the committee should attend first to recommendations that can be enacted within six months, and then turn to suggestions that will take longer to implement. The committee should specify in a written action plan the individuals, committees, or ad hoc task forces responsible for each activity, along with a time line. See Exhibit 2.5 for an example.

The retreat report and the draft action plan should be circulated to all trustees for comment and ultimately adopted by the board. At this point, the retreat planning committee can disband, and responsibility for follow-up can be assumed by the trusteeship committee or the executive committee.

GOAL SETTING

Retreats are one mechanism to help the board to establish goals *for the board*. Other avenues include board assessments, extended discussion at board meetings, and presidential transitions. Regardless of the source, the adoption of goals institutionalizes the expectation of growth and the habit of change and unites the board behind an effort to improve performance (much as Management by Objectives, MBO, serves the same purpose for employees and supervisors). Two trustees explained the value of goal setting:

> Since we began developing our board, we have set goals in a more regular and disciplined way. It has added focus. And the process of setting goals has improved our whole process as a board.

> Boards need to focus on goal setting, on what they're doing and what they should be doing. When there is a general mess, all you can do is talk. When you set specific goals, you can achieve them.

Some of the goals boards have adopted are:

- becoming better educated about key external trends affecting the institution
- developing a plan to groom future leadership for the board
- developing a board profile and a plan for altering the board's composition
- assessing the board's committee structure and determining how it can be modified to support the institution's strategy

- enhancing relations with a key constituency, such as professional staff members, faculty, or alumni
- formulating a process for assessing the board's performance

The corollary of the need to adopt goals is the need to assess goal attainment. "The board tried an evaluation that didn't work," a president recounted. "They were trying to evaluate themselves when they didn't know what they wanted to do." Thus, assessments that are tied to specific board goals—what might be termed Governance by Objectives—offer a more powerful way to institutionalize a culture amenable to change and dedicated to continuous improvement.

CONCLUSION

Most trustees will gladly commit time and expend energy to strengthen the board's performance, as long as a clear crosswalk exists between board development and desired outcomes, particularly improved institutional performance. Effective boards maintain that connection by continually reexamining their behavior and performance *in light of* institutional strategy and then devising appropriate responses. This approach allows the board to move beyond the search for a simple or quick fix toward the realization that board improvement comes about through a constant process of adaptation to altered circumstances. Progress will most likely take place when the chair, the president, or a subset of legitimately empowered trustees assumes responsibility for sustained attention to the way the board does business, and for determining whether the board should do business differently as institutional circumstances—and hence board circumstances—change. A trustee described the ingredients for success well:

> The president and chair are good strategic thinkers, so they've tried to move the board away from operations toward policy and strategy—what a board should be doing. The retreats we've had have helped us to be more strategic and cohesive. Our leaders actively seek to generate discussion on the board. The kinds of materials we have are more oriented toward larger issues. If you have materials and agendas that support the long view, and if you have informed and committed people as trustees, the board functions well—and it can get even better.

NOTES

1. For a fuller consideration of the arguments trustees and CEOs mount against board development, and the counterarguments, see Chapter 6.

2. We are indebted to our colleagues at The Cheswick Center for developing the original version of this list.

3. As professional facilitators, we acknowledge our bias, but we believe that retreats should, as a rule, be facilitated by outside experts.

Board Self-Assessment Questionnaire

Name of Organization _____

Thank you for participating in this study of non-profit organization boards. The following statements describe a variety of possible actions by boards. Some of the statements may represent your own experiences as a member of your board, while others may not. For each of the items, there are four possible choices. Please mark with a check (✓) the choice which most accurately describes your experience as a member of this board.

There are no "right" or "wrong" answers; your personal views are what is important. In order to ensure the anonymity of all responses, please do not put your name anywhere on the form. After you have completed all the items, please fold the form, insert it into the envelope provided, and drop it in the mail.

Thank you.

1. This board takes regular steps to keep informed about important trends in the larger environment that might affect the organization.	Strongly Agree	
	Agree	
	Disagree	
	Strongly Disagree	
2. I have participated in board discussions about what we should do differently as a result of a mistake the board made.	Strongly Agree	
	Agree	
	Disagree	
	Strongly Disagree	
3. I have had conversations with other members of this board regarding common interests we share outside this organization.	Strongly Agree	
	Agree	
	Disagree	
	Strongly Disagree	
4. We have had ad hoc committees or task forces co-chaired by a staff member and a board member.	Strongly Agree	
	Agree	
	Disagree	
	Strongly Disagree	
5. I have been in board meetings where it seemed that the subtleties of the issues we dealt with escaped the awareness of a number of the members.	Strongly Agree	
	Agree	
	Disagree	
	Strongly Disagree	

EXHIBIT 2.6

continued

6. Our board explicitly examines the "downside" or possible pitfalls of any important decision it is about to make.	Strongly Agree	
	Agree	
	Disagree	
	Strongly Disagree	
7. Orientation programs for new board members specifically include a segment about the organization's history and traditions.	Strongly Agree	
	Agree	
	Disagree	
	Strongly Disagree	
8. This board is more involved in trying to put out fires than in preparing for the future.	Strongly Agree	
	Agree	
	Disagree	
	Strongly Disagree	
9. The board sets clear organizational priorities for the year ahead.	Strongly Agree	
	Agree	
	Disagree	
	Strongly Disagree	
10. An annual report on this board's activities is prepared and distributed publicly.	Strongly Agree	
	Agree	
	Disagree	
	Strongly Disagree	
11. This board communicates its decisions to all those who are affected by them.	Strongly Agree	
	Agree	
	Disagree	
	Strongly Disagree	
12. At least once every two years, our board has a retreat or special session to examine our performance, how well we are doing as a board.	Strongly Agree	
	Agree	
	Disagree	
	Strongly Disagree	
13. Many of the issues that this board deals with seem to be separate tasks, unrelated to one another.	Strongly Agree	
	Agree	
	Disagree	
	Strongly Disagree	
14. In discussing key issues, it is not unusual for someone on the board to talk about what this organization stands for and how that is related to the matter at hand.	Strongly Agree	
	Agree	
	Disagree	
	Strongly Disagree	

EXHIBIT 2.6 (continued)

continued

15.	Values are seldom discussed explicitly at our board meetings.	Strongly Agree	
		Agree	
		Disagree	
		Strongly Disagree	

16.	If our board thinks that an important group or constituency is likely to disagree with an action we are considering, we will make sure we learn how they feel before we actually make the decision.	Strongly Agree	
		Agree	
		Disagree	
		Strongly Disagree	

17.	Differences of opinion in board decisions are more often settled by vote than by more discussion.	Strongly Agree	
		Agree	
		Disagree	
		Strongly Disagree	

18.	There are individuals on this board who are identified as responsible for maintaining channels of communication with specific key community leaders.	Strongly Agree	
		Agree	
		Disagree	
		Strongly Disagree	

19.	This board delays action until an issue becomes urgent or critical.	Strongly Agree	
		Agree	
		Disagree	
		Strongly Disagree	

20.	This board periodically sets aside time to learn more about important issues facing organizations like the one we govern.	Strongly Agree	
		Agree	
		Disagree	
		Strongly Disagree	

21.	I can recall an occasion when the board acknowledged its responsibility for an ill-advised decision.	Strongly Agree	
		Agree	
		Disagree	
		Strongly Disagree	

22.	This board has formed ad hoc committees or task forces that include staff as well as board members.	Strongly Agree	
		Agree	
		Disagree	
		Strongly Disagree	

23.	This board is as attentive to how it reaches conclusions as it is to what is decided.	Strongly Agree	
		Agree	
		Disagree	
		Strongly Disagree	

EXHIBIT 2.6 (continued)

continued

24. The decisions of this board on one issue tend to influence what we do about other issues that come before us.	Strongly Agree	
	Agree	
	Disagree	
	Strongly Disagree	

25. Most people on this board tend to rely on observation and informal discussions to learn about their role and responsibilities.	Strongly Agree	
	Agree	
	Disagree	
	Strongly Disagree	

26. I find it easy to identify the key issues that this board faces.	Strongly Agree	
	Agree	
	Disagree	
	Strongly Disagree	

27. When faced with an important issue, the board often "brainstorms" and tries to generate a whole list of creative approaches or solutions to the problem.	Strongly Agree	
	Agree	
	Disagree	
	Strongly Disagree	

28. When a new member joins this board, we make sure that someone serves as a mentor to help this person learn the ropes.	Strongly Agree	
	Agree	
	Disagree	
	Strongly Disagree	

29. I have been in board meetings where explicit attention was given to the concerns of the community.	Strongly Agree	
	Agree	
	Disagree	
	Strongly Disagree	

30. I rarely disagree openly with other members in board meetings.	Strongly Agree	
	Agree	
	Disagree	
	Strongly Disagree	

31. I have participated in board discussions about the effectiveness of our performance.	Strongly Agree	
	Agree	
	Disagree	
	Strongly Disagree	

32. At our board meetings, there is at least as much dialogue among members as there is between members and administrators.	Strongly Agree	
	Agree	
	Disagree	
	Strongly Disagree	

EXHIBIT 2.6 (continued)

continued

33. When issues come before our board, they are seldom framed in a way that enables members to see the connections between the matter at hand and the organization's overall strategy.	Strongly Agree	
	Agree	
	Disagree	
	Strongly Disagree	

34. I have participated in discussions with new members about the roles and responsibilities of a board member.	Strongly Agree	
	Agree	
	Disagree	
	Strongly Disagree	

35. This board has made a key decision that I believe to be inconsistent with the mission of this organization.	Strongly Agree	
	Agree	
	Disagree	
	Strongly Disagree	

36. The leadership of this board typically goes out of its way to make sure that all members have the same information on important issues.	Strongly Agree	
	Agree	
	Disagree	
	Strongly Disagree	

37. This board has adopted some explicit goals for itself, distinct from goals it has for the total organization.	Strongly Agree	
	Agree	
	Disagree	
	Strongly Disagree	

38. The board often requests that a decision be postponed until further information can be obtained.	Strongly Agree	
	Agree	
	Disagree	
	Strongly Disagree	

39. The board periodically requests information on the morale of the professional staff.	Strongly Agree	
	Agree	
	Disagree	
	Strongly Disagree	

40. I have participated in board discussions about what we can learn from a mistake we have made.	Strongly Agree	
	Agree	
	Disagree	
	Strongly Disagree	

41. Our board meetings tend to focus more on current concerns than on preparing for the future.	Strongly Agree	
	Agree	
	Disagree	
	Strongly Disagree	

EXHIBIT 2.6 (continued)

continued

42. At least once a year, this board asks that the executive director articulate his/her vision for the organization's future and strategies to realize that vision.	Strongly Agree	
	Agree	
	Disagree	
	Strongly Disagree	

43. I have been present in board meetings where discussions of the history and mission of the organization were key factors in reaching a conclusion on a problem.	Strongly Agree	
	Agree	
	Disagree	
	Strongly Disagree	

44. I have never received feedback on my performance as a member of this board.	Strongly Agree	
	Agree	
	Disagree	
	Strongly Disagree	

45. It is apparent from the comments of some of our board members that they do not understand the mission of the organization very well.	Strongly Agree	
	Agree	
	Disagree	
	Strongly Disagree	

46. This board has on occasion evaded responsibility for some important issue facing the organization.	Strongly Agree	
	Agree	
	Disagree	
	Strongly Disagree	

47. Before reaching a decision on important issues, this board usually requests input from persons likely to be affected by the decision.	Strongly Agree	
	Agree	
	Disagree	
	Strongly Disagree	

48. There have been occasions where the board itself has acted in ways inconsistent with the organization's deepest values.	Strongly Agree	
	Agree	
	Disagree	
	Strongly Disagree	

49. This board relies on the natural emergence of leaders, rather than trying explicitly to cultivate future leaders for the board.	Strongly Agree	
	Agree	
	Disagree	
	Strongly Disagree	

50. This board often discusses where the organization should be headed five or more years into the future.	Strongly Agree	
	Agree	
	Disagree	
	Strongly Disagree	

EXHIBIT 2.6 (continued)

continued

51. New members are provided with a detailed explanation of this organization's mission when they join this board.	Strongly Agree	
	Agree	
	Disagree	
	Strongly Disagree	

52. This board does not allocate organizational funds for the purpose of board education and development.	Strongly Agree	
	Agree	
	Disagree	
	Strongly Disagree	

53. Other board members have important information that I lack on key issues.	Strongly Agree	
	Agree	
	Disagree	
	Strongly Disagree	

54. Recommendations from the administration are usually accepted with little questioning in board meetings.	Strongly Agree	
	Agree	
	Disagree	
	Strongly Disagree	

55. At times this board has appeared unaware of the impact its decisions will have within our service community.	Strongly Agree	
	Agree	
	Disagree	
	Strongly Disagree	

56. Within the past year, this board has reviewed the organization's strategies for attaining its long-term goals.	Strongly Agree	
	Agree	
	Disagree	
	Strongly Disagree	

57. This board reviews the organization's mission at least once every five years.	Strongly Agree	
	Agree	
	Disagree	
	Strongly Disagree	

58. This board has conducted an explicit examination of its roles and responsibilities.	Strongly Agree	
	Agree	
	Disagree	
	Strongly Disagree	

59. I am able to speak my mind on key issues without fear that I will be ostracized by some members of this board.	Strongly Agree	
	Agree	
	Disagree	
	Strongly Disagree	

EXHIBIT 2.6 (continued)

continued

60. This board tries to avoid issues that are ambiguous and complicated.	Strongly Agree	
	Agree	
	Disagree	
	Strongly Disagree	

61. The administration rarely reports to the board on the concerns of those the organization serves.	Strongly Agree	
	Agree	
	Disagree	
	Strongly Disagree	

62. I have been in board meetings where the discussion focused on identifying or overcoming the organization's weaknesses.	Strongly Agree	
	Agree	
	Disagree	
	Strongly Disagree	

63. One of the reasons I joined this board was that I believe strongly in the values of this organization.	Strongly Agree	
	Agree	
	Disagree	
	Strongly Disagree	

64. This board does not recognize special events in the lives of its members.	Strongly Agree	
	Agree	
	Disagree	
	Strongly Disagree	

65. The board faces many policy questions that do not have clear answers.	Strongly Agree	
	Agree	
	Disagree	
	Strongly Disagree	

66. The board discusses events and trends in the larger environment that may present specific opportunities for this organization.	Strongly Agree	
	Agree	
	Disagree	
	Strongly Disagree	

67. Former members of this board have participated in special events designed to convey to new members the organization's history and values.	Strongly Agree	
	Agree	
	Disagree	
	Strongly Disagree	

68. This board provides biographical information that helps members get to know one another better.	Strongly Agree	
	Agree	
	Disagree	
	Strongly Disagree	

EXHIBIT 2.6 (continued)

continued

69. This board seeks information and advice from leaders of other similar organizations.	Strongly Agree	
	Agree	
	Disagree	
	Strongly Disagree	

70. This board makes explicit use of the long range priorities of this organization in dealing with current issues.	Strongly Agree	
	Agree	
	Disagree	
	Strongly Disagree	

71. This board understands the norms of the professions working in this organization.	Strongly Agree	
	Agree	
	Disagree	
	Strongly Disagree	

72. Members of this board seldom attend social events sponsored by this organization.	Strongly Agree	
	Agree	
	Disagree	
	Strongly Disagree	

73. More than half of this board's time is spent in discussions of issues of importance to the organization's long-range future.	Strongly Agree	
	Agree	
	Disagree	
	Strongly Disagree	

EXHIBIT 2.6 (continued)

CHAPTER

Transforming Trustees into a Board

Some trustees and presidents are deeply skeptical about the ability of a board *as a board* to accomplish anything. To them, the board *qua* board exists only to provide legitimacy to the actions of the individuals and subgroups in which the board's real power and competence reside. This view, which reflects an American conviction that only individuals produce results, gains reinforcement from the tendency of institutions to select successful individuals as trustees. "I'm an entrepreneur, a lone wolf. I don't think much about teams," declared a university trustee. However, Lorsch concluded from a study of corporate boards that, apart from legal authority, "Group cohesion is [a board's] most significant . . . power source" (1989, 169–70). CEOs have knowledge, time, control of the agenda, and other sources of influence. A fragmented board, Lorsch maintains, will easily be overpowered by such strength. Similarly, Yale professor Clayton Alderfer asserts that the board's "effective authority," or "legitimate right to do work," depends directly on group dynamics, "the invisible director on corporate boards" (1986, 47).

Consistent with these views, we believe that on the most effective boards, trustees, as a group, are the central force. This chapter discusses the advantages of a cohesive board and considers how a collection of individuals can be transformed into an effective board of trustees. Essentially, the task is to withstand, by deliberate, sustained attention to the group, the natural tendency of talented, and usually committed, individuals to gravitate toward solo service to the institution. The most useful counterforces are meaningful work driven by collectively established goals, socialization, information, and careful cultivation and selection of board members and board leaders.

INDIVIDUALS IN ACTION

Skepticism among trustees and presidents about boards derives partly from doubts about the fundamental assumptions that underlie the concept of trusteeship: that a large group of nonresident amateurs, infrequently convened, can assume responsibility for a complex, ongoing enterprise managed by resident professionals. In response to this predicament, many trustees render individual service to the institution, based on their expertise. For such board members, this *personal* contribution defines trusteeship. One trustee, disturbed at a staff recommendation to refinance the institution's debt as zero-coupon bonds stated: "I had an analyst at my business put it on the computer. A guy like me who has some expertise is obligated to make sure mistakes aren't made." He added, "A lot of times I'll see a problem. I'll document it and write a long memo to the chair, the president, or the staff. That's all I'll have to say." At another institution, after a search for a new president failed, a trustee, who was a partner in an executive search firm, basically expropriated the process. As described by another trustee, "He volunteered a couple of months pro bono. He knew how to find good candidates and how to keep things confidential. That's competence in action, not just talk."

Some trustees pursue special interests or relationships through membership on the board. One board member reported, "The chair of the buildings and grounds committee drove the president crazy in efforts to improve the campus." At another institution, where the president urged the board to support a controversial administrative appointment, "One trustee took it upon himself to call faculty to find out what they thought, and the faculty mobilized against the appointment." An extreme example of individual competence in action was the college trustee who said, "I'm the CFO of a large organization, and so I got involved in the college's finances. Several years ago, I started putting together the college's annual budgets."

RELIANCE ON SUBGROUPS

"We probably haven't had the best organized and functioning board, but we have had a handful of real leaders. That's the essence of good board performance," declared the chairman of a college board. Surely, many trustees can identify with that description of trusteeship.

For some board members, reliance on subgroups, especially the executive committee, seems to be a necessary evil. Board size, lack of time, geography, and infrequency of meetings are viewed as insurmountable barriers to involvement by the full board, as these comments from five trustees of different boards illustrate:

Things move too fast to keep everyone up to date.

One of the difficulties for me is the sense of ownership. The board meets so seldom, and we have 50-plus members. Our contact with the day-to-day is relatively infrequent.

We can't just bop over for events or stay easily in touch.

The board is too big. The numbers alone make it hard to function as a unit.

You can't take the time to keep everyone updated on every detail if you're going to succeed in getting the job done. . . . It's results that count.

For others, the essential problem with boards as groups pertains less to insurmountable barriers to broader involvement than to a Darwinian view that the "fittest" trustees should rightfully exercise greater control and wield more power than less gifted colleagues on the board, a perspective stated matter-of-factly by the chairman of a university board:

What about those trustees who are outside the loop? It doesn't matter to me. There are those who contribute and make things happen and those who don't. That's life. You never find a board at its best in a formal meeting. The key is the power brokers, those who decide the university's future direction. You know, it's like you learn in a large family: If you don't go for the potatoes, there won't be any left. That's the way it is in a corporate environment, and that's the way it is on a board.

WHY EMPOWER THE BOARD?

Given the inherent difficulty of including and empowering the entire board, why bother? The answer for most members and leaders of effective boards rests on four premises.

1. The corporate concept of the *group* as the decision-making entity constitutes a core value and fundamental tenet of trusteeship. "There's a certain collective consciousness," declared a particularly insightful and reflective board chairman, "that has to be tapped. It's somewhat metaphysical. It's different from having a set of individuals in separate telephone booths participating when they want to. The board as a whole must have a different process."
2. Properly constituted and engaged, the group will make better decisions than individuals or a subgroup. As members of an especially effective board observed, "If everyone participates, theoretically you should have a better product, a better decision." "We're trying to find ways to make sure that we draw on the variety of perspectives among our members and

even to stretch those perspectives so we'll have the very best ideas for responding to the issues we face."

3. Inclusiveness can be an antidote to the groupthink that sometimes afflicts subgroups of like-minded trustees. "We have a mayor who surrounds himself with clones, people very much like himself. . . . He doesn't have anyone who will say, 'That is stupid. We need to rethink that.'"

4. The personal commitment and talent of trustees can be secured only if board members feel equitably treated. "The only way to get the best out of everyone is to hear what each one has to say." Trustees outside the power loop will be angry, alienated, and exasperated, as evidenced by the comments of three trustees, on different boards, yet linked by a common frustration:

> Meetings tend to be dominated by a few loud voices from a small in-group, especially those on the executive committee. It's a little closed club of WASP males who give lip service to inclusiveness but don't really practice it. It's nice, I know, to have all that control, but it's not good for the rest of the board.

> I'm one of only three females on this board, and I'm really tired of trying to open up attention to others—women and minorities—who have not been heard by the board.

> Decisions are being made on the golf course, and other people are losing interest in participating. They are reluctant to vocalize their concerns because it would be very dangerous to turn off the heavy hitters on the board with the money and the access to money.

More than one college trustee has articulated the paradox in which "the president and the officers handle more and more of the decisions while, at the same time, the college is calling for broader expertise on the board. How can you build a capable board without granting real authority to the group?"

BECOMING A BOARD

In order to transform trustees into a board, the institution must overcome the very real and powerful forces that, unless actively and consistently countered, tend to place most power in the hands of a few trustees and the president. "Good performance doesn't result just from having strong or the right people on the board. And you don't get there overnight."

Cohesive and inclusive boards are inherently untidy and frequently unpredictable. Involving more people and being susceptible to their influence requires a tolerance for tension, conflict, error, and ambiguity. This circumstance offends the need of many board members for order and control, and it helps explain the prevalence of individual activity and the dominance by subgroups that characterize fragmented boards. "The chair is very structured and organized. He is not about to be caught by surprise. As the CEO of a Fortune 500 company, he works in a structured way. Some say this means everything will be predetermined before the board meets. Others say we are now better organized." In fact, one of this chair's first acts was to establish an "advisory committee" of the board's four officers to meet monthly with the president—a move other trustees, including some members of the previously powerful executive committee, saw as an attempt to limit the number of influential members on the board.

Contrast this action with the practice of another board for which open discussion and decision making within the entire board are the norm: "If there is a hard question that comes up, for example, tenure—which is a very sensitive issue—the whole board discusses it. Another board, not as good as ours, would discuss it in a small group first and try to control everything. It wouldn't be as collegial. It wouldn't be as consensus building. This board is just not 'top down.'" A member of another inclusive board noted, "We have had the patience to sort through, and talk, and worry, and reflect, so that we make the right institutional response. We've clearly frustrated some people by taking the time to do this, but most of us think it's important to build a sense of trust and move along together."

Members of cohesive boards describe the ability to disagree openly within the board as evidence of good board performance.

> Open dissent is good because you avoid frustrations down the road. Seething is not good. You have to see that open dissent does occur and that people see that it doesn't breach a friendship or harm the institution.

> Conflicts or problems can be a cementing factor. When we work together on a problem, people's hidden talents come out. Once that happens, you know a person, and you know you can count on that person.

> The best way to have constructive dissent is to have constructive board members—people who are willing to listen *and* speak their minds.

> I evaluate the board by the quality of conversations at the meetings. Are people stimulated and engaged? Are they arguing constructively? If they're not that engaged, they're not being effective.

Commitment

Board effectiveness cannot be expected or attained unless trustees are sufficiently attached to the institution and to one another to assume ownership of the board's actions and performance. Along these lines, one member of a very effective board cited the complex of "webs and relationships among members of this board" as a key to its dedication.

In earlier research, we concluded that the more numerous the connections prospective college trustees already had to the institution (e.g., as alumni, parents of students, or members of the sponsoring denomination), the deeper their commitment to serve and the more effective their board (Taylor, Chait, and Holland 1991). Commitment may, of course, also be learned through *positive* experience as a trustee. Whatever the specific sources, engagement in the board's work as a trustee ultimately depends on a deep loyalty to the institution and a belief that one's contributions to the board's work affect the institution.

Members of effective boards understand that commitment (or the lack thereof) will greatly affect board performance.

> Trustees need to understand that they are the *owners* of the institution, not just monitors for it. There has to be a total commitment to the institution, just like you'd have unlimited liability as a general partner in a private firm—just that magnitude of commitment. With that perspective, a trustee is motivated to be active, to contribute, to learn and grow, to actively engage in finding solutions to major problems.

Contrast this declaration with the trustee who confessed, "There is no ownership by the board of the institution. It's not *let's* do this or that. We really have an extraordinary composition on the board. It's not a problem of individual capability."

Effective boards do not restrict the obligation to be committed and the right to be influential to an in-group of experienced trustees. Unlike fragmented boards that view trustee passivity as an opportunity to concentrate power in the hands of a few, inclusive boards find disengagement of individual trustees to be disruptive. "Collegiality is supported by seeing everyone shoulder the work and carry it out well. It is undermined when you see some people coasting or dragging things down." The necessity of involvement extends to new trustees as well. "Giving new members responsibility fast maintains their interest. The old idea of a new member just sort of watching for a year is a vote for the status quo."

Meaningful Work

The nature of a board's work and the extent of the trustees' involvement exerts enormous influence over group cohesiveness and commitment. Trustees must view the issues before the board as important and the board's involvement as central to the institution's ability to resolve those issues. The more important trustees perceive the work to be, the more trustees will feel influential and committed. The cycle proceeds from initial interest and commitment to hard work on behalf of the institution, which further reinforces commitment.

Important matters engross trustees and offer a powerful reason to participate. "The board was at its best when we were working on the strategic plan
and defining a niche. What made this work was the important nature of the
work itself and the process. We saw the board really labor and form opinions
collectively."

Literature and rhetoric to the contrary, many boards, *as boards*, feel anything but essential. Certainly, boards carry symbolic weight, receive information, hear reports, and discuss matters, especially in committees. These activities are more than empty rituals. Yet, only a minority of trustees assert with
conviction that the board's work (as opposed to the staff's work) is absolutely
vital to institutional success. If trustees see the board as marginal and unproductive, important primarily as a backstop or token, few will make an earnest
commitment to the group.

Active involvement is pivotal to group formation and preservation. "This is
a participating board, not one where you lend your name and then go play golf.
The expectation is that you will do more than just show up. It means reading
all the materials, participating in discussions, doing some outside reading, and
having respect for everyone—being collegial and cohesive." This is different
from a board included on matters of moment at the whim of the "real" leaders
and, then, more to be informed than to be consulted. With effort, the
transformation from players to team can occur through meaningful work.
"Before, as a staffer, I would notice that trustees would be talked at during
most of our meetings. There was no board input into the data they were given.
They made decisions on things they didn't understand or care about. We've
come a long way in getting them involved. Now their deliberations really mean
something." And, we would observe, this board has congealed.

Social Interaction

We do not mean to condemn a board to an existence of "all work and no
play"—or the converse, for that matter. Obviously, the board must strike an
acceptable balance. We wish to suggest only that neither be neglected, as the
two are not unrelated.

Social interactions among trustees enhance collegiality and inclusiveness,
which, in turn, infuse a board's work. As one trustee remarked, "We're all
animals, and we live in packs. You need to know who you're running with." In
fact, sociable boards, also engaged in significant work, frequently discover that
social time and work time meld together. "The board meets and works hard
and then we have a dinner where we all get together. The dinner gives you an
opportunity for social exchange but more importantly an opportunity for
exchange about issues facing the college." "Our meetings are so collegial they
look like social events, and our social events always involve some discussion of
work. There's no dividing line."

Social events are the most obvious way to enhance fellowship within the board, and inclusive boards schedule such events for almost every meeting and sometimes between meetings. "There are lots of social occasions. The president and his wife entertain frequently. They often have groups in, including members of the board. We have a constant association with one another and with the institution." "This board is open and very collegial. Everyone knows everyone. Sometimes it's hard to get meetings started; they come early so they can visit with each other. It's hard to get them to come back from breaks. We have a social occasion at each meeting. Sometimes I think some of them come just for that!"

As conducive as trustee receptions and dinners are to uniting a group, some institutions go further. One college, with a predominantly local board, invites all trustees to an informal monthly luncheon with the president to raise topics of interest. Other boards have organized trips intended to educate trustees and, just as important, to enhance group cohesion. The trustees of a Roman Catholic college financed a board trip to Europe to tour sites and hear lectures related to the college's founding religious order. The board of a seminary travelled, also at personal expense, with the institution's archaeologist president to visit the Middle East and trace the roots of Christianity.

Social events should also be an integral component of board retreats (see also "Board Retreats," Chapter 2), although we sometimes encounter some initial resistance to the idea among trustees determined to "use every minute wisely and productively." Yet, almost without exception, every board has greatly enjoyed the activities, usually planned for the late afternoon or after dinner, that were designed to enhance collegiality. The shared laughter or the tales of someone's youth provide a common bond that often outlives the retreat.

One board of a liberal arts college offered multiple social events during a three-hour respite set aside for recreation during their retreat. Activities included volleyball, a nature walk with a geologist, and a book discussion guided by a professor. Another board has established a tradition of a trustee golf tournament as an important team builder. Custom dictates that even nongolfers walk or ride along and join in the banter (and the search for lost balls). Trustees of a major university travelled together in a bus to a retreat site two hours away and then returned to campus in time to attend the school's basketball game. Being together in this unaccustomed way, sharing box lunches and camaraderie, set the stage for open communication at the retreat and for continuing discussions afterwards.

Equal Access to Information

Board members without equal access to information may not feel or act like equal members of the group. Trustees are never more deflated or distanced than on occasions when they learn third hand or late in the day important information already known to most other board members. Cohesive boards consider equal access to information indispensable to board effectiveness because, as one trustee astutely observed, "the more informed you are, the more you have a sense of ownership." Members of other boards concur:

> There's a deep commitment to having everyone understand the needs of the institution and engaged in working on them. No one is left out of the loop; everyone gets full information on everything. We've stopped leaving things in the hands of a few, while everyone else is in the dark.

> The goal is to provide everyone with the opportunity to hear and see the same things.

> The committees meet separately, but all the minutes go to everyone.

> In times of crisis, we use conference calls to keep everyone informed.

Presidents and board chairs are essential for keeping *all* trustees abreast of important news and developments, whether through newsletters, phone calls, personal notes, or informal conversations over breakfast or lunch. One college president has made a personal commitment to telephone each board member at least once, and preferably twice, a semester; another, a community college president with only six trustees, speaks to each one weekly. These calls enable the president to update trustees on issues of special concern and to cultivate effective working relationships with each trustee. This may enable the president to avoid the common problem described by the former head of another college: "If I had it to do over again, I might have spent more time interacting with the trustees who were not in the inner circle. I spent a lot of time talking with the inner circle group, and it is possible I could have developed a closer relationship with some of the other trustees in ways that would have been useful to the board and the college." On several boards, the chair plays a similar role in a similar fashion: keeping all trustees informed through newsletters, phone calls, or informal luncheons.

These practices, plus several discussed in Chapter 5 (e.g., committees of the whole and executive sessions), help unite a board with a common base of information and a collective sense of responsibility for the board's full range of duties. Too often, the alternative is a balkanized board, divided by differential information, mutually exclusive territories, and little commerce among members.

Using Trustee Talent and Expertise

Effective boards imbue the group with authority *and* use trustees' individual expertise, connections, judgment, and interests in pursuit of collective goals. Trustees do find individual work satisfying, and they do appreciate the opportunity to use their talents and professional expertise to solve problems for the institution. "Everyone on the board was chosen for the variety of their skills and experiences, and we want to take advantage of these."

Paradoxically, inclusive boards find that the most helpful individual contributions sometimes come from trustees who are not experts on the subject at hand. "We want everyone's input, whether it is in their area of expertise or not. In fact, we often get the best advice from board members outside their area of expertise." Such individuals can ask "naive" questions that supposed "sophisticates" may be too embarrassed to pose, and introduce perspectives that prompt new lines of inquiry and creativity. In fact, for this very reason, one seminary board traditionally chooses someone *not* from a business or financial background to chair the finance committee. The current finance chair, a retired trial attorney, explained, "I make it a point to ask all the dumb questions that might be on other trustees' minds. And I figure that if the budget can be explained to me in a way that makes sense, then everyone else will understand it too."

Unless invited and organized by the board, individual trustee activity will undermine rather than support the board's cohesion and authority. On one college campus, the president and the trusteeship committee proposed a set of individual trustee goals based on each member's specific interests, skills, and contacts. For example, a local attorney was asked to help in a financial negotiation with another college in the area; an alumnus trustee living in a large city 500 miles away was asked to assume four or five local speaking engagements for the fundraising campaign; a trustee with professional expertise in art was asked to help organize an arts advisory committee and a "friend of the arts" program; and a prominent business person was asked to provide internships for one or more students. "Having a group of people [the trusteeship committee] who think about the contributions each individual trustee can make is very useful." The conversations where trustees were asked to assume these assignments produced some surprises: "On a one-to-one basis, you sometimes find they have a wonderful, hidden idea about something they might want to undertake for the college. You don't want them to take on some maverick operation, so this is a great way to identify and funnel their ideas back to the group."

Other boards ask each trustee to set specific annual goals. Some boards use a relatively informal process, others a more elaborate approach. At a recent retreat, a trustee who had been designated as the facilitator of a discussion session spontaneously invited fellow board members to suggest specific goals for the board and for individual trustees to adopt that would advance the institution. One board member pledged to host a reception within two months for local alumni. In a more formal process, one university's trusteeship committee sends a letter and goal-setting form to each board member every

September (see Exhibit 3.1). Trustees set personal goals that will make them more valuable board members and then conduct a self-assessment at the end of the year.

A Goal-Setting Process for Individual Trustees

Letter from the Committee on Trustees

Dear (Trustee):

The Committee on Trustees of _____ College is grateful for your continuing service to the board and the college. As you know, the committee asks trustees to participate annually in a written "Performance Goals and Self-Evaluation" exercise. At the beginning of the year, each trustee is asked to establish personal goals and to request from the administration information or assistance that you may need to enhance your performance as a board member during the coming year. At the end of the year, each of us will be asked to conduct a self-evaluation, based on the goals we set earlier.

Enclosed is a form that we ask you to use in developing your goals for the year. Please complete the form and return it to me in the enclosed envelope, retaining a copy for your files. Members of the board and/or the staff will contact you about both your plans to help the college and about any assistance you may have requested from the college. At the end of the year, the Committee on Trustees will return your form to you, along with a self-evaluation sheet, and ask that you assess your own performance.

Your participation in this effort is much appreciated. Please call me or any other member of the Committee on Trustees if you have questions.

Sincerely,

(Chair, Committee on Trustees)

Personal Performance Goals and Self-Evaluation, 1996–97

In order to fulfill my responsibilities and to stay informed as a member of the _____ College Board of Trustees, and to increase my understanding of my responsibilities, I agree to meet the following goals during the coming year:

1. Attend all regular meetings of the board and of the committees to which I am assigned.
2. Participate in the Annual Fund and other giving opportunities, to my potential.
3. In addition to the above, I agree to involve myself in the life of the College by accomplishing as many as possible of the following goals, consistent with my interests and personal circumstances. (Circle the goals you select, and add in the spaces provided any others that you would like to pursue.)
   a. Identify 3 new donor prospects (individual, corporate, or foundation).
   b. Participate in the cultivation and/or solicitation of 3 new donors (individual, corporate, or foundation).

EXHIBIT 3.1

continued

c. Make personal contact by letter or phone with 3 prospective students and 10 accepted students.

d. Host, organize, or participate in an event for admissions or advancement.

e. Attend at least two on-campus, nonboard events.

f. Attend at least one college-sponsored off-campus event, such as an alumni meeting.

g. Consult for at least one day with the college in my area of expertise.

h. Teach a class or make a special presentation to a class or audience at the college.

i. Advise a student organization, department, or group.

j. Attend and/or represent the College at a minimum of one meeting or conference relating to trusteeship or higher education.

k. Through my business or professional contacts, recruit on campus, hire, or provide job counseling to at least one student or alumnus seeking employment.

l. Other activities not listed above:

_____

_____

_____

What support or information will you need from the board or staff in order to accomplish these goals? _____

_____

_____

_____

_____
Signature and Date

Self-Assessment
(To be completed a year after goals are set)

Please review the goals you set for yourself as a trustee. Were you able to accomplish your goals? What barriers did you face, if any? How can the board and staff help ensure that you and other trustees become even more successful in the coming year? Please add any comments about the goal-setting process itself.

_____

_____

_____

_____
Signature and Date

EXHIBIT 3.1 (continued)

Irrespective of the process used to elicit individual trustee involvement, "The main advantage," summarized one board chair, "is that trustees have much more of a sense of their specific assignments, as opposed to being a general trustee at large. I think having individual assignments has tightened people's sense of responsibility."

BOARD BUILDING

Like a functional building, an effective board reflects the combination of careful planning and skillful construction to meet specific needs. The process starts with the selection of new members and includes orientation, education, socialization, and evaluation of trustees and the board.

Trustee Selection

Too often, as one trustee lamented, the tactic boards use to select new members is to "add as many friends as you can in the hope that some of them will turn out to be helpful. That's a poor approach. You need to be thoughtful about what sorts of skills the board really needs; some criteria for selection that are based on the real needs of the institution and the board itself." Many boards understate the seriousness of the commitment desired from trustees by pledging to prospects, often affluent and prominent individuals with no strong ties to the institution, that they "won't have to do much." Typically, such boards assume that commitment will emerge naturally once the individual starts to attend meetings. More often than not, however, these "letterhead trustees" disappoint by doing precisely what they were asked to do—not much. Capable people with real capacity for commitment are apt to be discouraged by being told that the board will demand little of them. As one trustee said, "I'm too busy to sit around doing nothing." In order to be more explicit about trustee qualifications, one board adopted a formal statement of qualifications for board membership to guide consideration of prospective members (see Exhibit 3.2).

Effective boards look for opportunities to evaluate and test the commitment and capabilities of prospective trustees *before* these individuals are invited to join the board. The trusteeship committee and staff at one college did extensive research on potential board members, not only to ascertain financial capacity, but also to learn about previous service to the college, possible competing obligations, personality, and working style. Typically, the college's board approaches alumni as prospects, and most are well known to at least one or two members of the trusteeship committee, usually through the alumni association.

Qualifications for Board Membership

It is the objective of the Committee on Trusteeship to create a diverse membership for the board, including representation of age, gender, and racial diversity; areas of expertise; geographical distribution; college relationship; financial position; church affiliation; and length of service. The Committee on Trusteeship also considers the optimal size of the board, financial expectations for members, and all of the other qualifications deemed appropriate for board membership.

Candidate Profiles

In order to maximize the number of active, contributing members of the board, the board has adopted the following four profiles describing those most suitable for membership:

- **Candidate with great promise.** This person is a high achiever in his/her occupation and 10–20 years into his/her career. Some in this category are expected to acquire or have access to significant wealth as they move forward in their careers. Others may not be expected to possess great wealth, but will be considered because of their commitment to the college, special talent(s), or willingness to give exceptional service to the realization of the college's mission. Normally, the promising young professional will be capable of only modest financial support in the early years of trusteeship. Candidates in this category will nearly always be alumni of the college.
- **Candidate with national reputation.** This person is one with a national reputation in his/her profession and thereby is expected to bring national visibility to the college through his/her trusteeship.
- **Candidate with significant financial resources.** This person is normally an alumnus/alumna of the college who is likely 20–30 years into his/her career. He/she is chosen because of the anticipated ability to make long-term, significant financial contributions. In particular, large annual fund contributions are expected, as well as major support for capital programs through significant gifts of cash and/or estate gifts. Giving of these candidates may not be sacrificial, but should always be significant.
- **Candidate with special expertise or perspective.** This person brings special expertise or perspective because of personal or professional affiliation. Included in this category are educators, clergy, and recent graduates, along with some members of traditionally underrepresented groups.

For all categories, the board seeks men and women strongly committed to the mission of the college who represent diverse views and opinions and who come from diverse backgrounds.

Trustee Responsibilities: The Three T's

Time. A trustee should share generously of his/her time to assist in promoting the legitimate interests and aspirations of the college within his/her sphere of influence. The commitment of time includes board and board committee meetings but is not limited to these. Article I, Section 3 of the board bylaws states: "A

EXHIBIT 3.2

continued

board member who fails to attend at least 50 percent of the regularly scheduled board and standing committee meetings during a three-year term shall by such failure have resigned from the board and relinquished the seat on the board, effective immediately."

Talent. A trustee should commit his/her talents to assist in making this a liberal arts college of nationally recognized excellence.

Treasure. A trustee should give as he/she is able, to support the educational mission of the college. All trustees are expected to give at the President's Club level or above. It is hoped that the college will be the trustee's principal charitable interest. Candidates will be informed of the present level of commitment by current members of the board.

EXHIBIT 3.2 (continued)

The college's president and/or another member of the trusteeship committee assume responsibility for cultivating each candidate under serious consideration. The specific steps are tailored to the candidate's circumstances. The prospective trustee might be invited to lunch with the president, to campus for a special event, or to a trustee's home for dinner; the candidate might even be asked to join a special committee or participate in a visit with a prospective donor. In one or two cases, a consultant who has worked with the board has been enlisted to talk to the prospect about the board's operating style and strengths. By the time the "ask" is made, the prospective trustee knows a great deal about the board's expectations, and the board has first-hand assurance of the individual's capabilities and commitment.

Another institution, which established boards of visitors to advise and advance particular schools within the university, regards those committees as "fertile areas to select new board members." The experience of working together reveals individuals with sufficient commitment to the institution and the ability to work within a group.

The charter of the board of visitors for the university's college of business administration (Exhibit 3.3) illustrates the features that make these advisory groups good tests of capacity for trusteeship: significant responsibilities, substantive agendas, and access to senior staff and the board. For the same reasons, alumni bodies, parents' councils, capital campaign committees, and special task forces also can be sources of demonstrable talent for trusteeship.

One very effective board, committed to inclusiveness, believes that all trustees should have a say in the appointment of new board members in order to reinforce the collective nature of trusteeship. Once the trusteeship committee concludes that a candidate should be considered seriously for membership, but before any final decision, the name comes before the full board for preliminary discussion. "The board has never rejected a candidate formally nominated by the trusteeship committee, but we have had proposed trustees derailed before that point. We have safeguards built in so that anyone who may have objections has time to voice them."

Board of Visitors Charter, College of Business Administration

The purpose of the board of visitors is to assist the College of Business Administration, advise the university board of trustees, and to assure that the college offers the highest quality in business education. Quality is to be assured through the board's evaluation of the college's planning, progress, and activities, with an eye toward fulfilling the educational needs of emerging and continuing business professionals, ensuring that they are prepared for future success in the interdependent, competitive, and global society.

Responsibilities of the Board of Visitors

- Advocate the mission, goals, and objectives of the College of Business Administration to external constituencies.
- Introduce the dean of the College of Business Administration and appropriate faculty members to the local and national business community.
- Support college activities by sharing knowledge and expertise by serving as guest speakers, mentors, and assisting in providing faculty and student internships.
- Assist in soliciting corporations, foundations, or individuals, when appropriate for the College of Business Administration.
- Provide personal and/or corporate support.

Appointment

Each board of visitors member is appointed for a three-year term with a maximum of two consecutive terms. Normally, between 10 and 15 members will form the board. Three appointments are made by the board of trustees and the rest by the president, upon recommendation of the dean and approval of the board of trustees. Nominations are broadly solicited from faculty, staff, friends, alumni, and trustees.

Meetings

Two full meetings are held each year. Committees of the board of visitors meet more frequently, pursuant to their assignments. There are committees for each program (BBA and MBA), and others as defined by the board of visitors and the dean.

Relation to the Board of Trustees

The board of visitors is not a policy-making body. Its role is to assist in the development of the college and to assist the board of trustees in evaluating the progress of the college. The chair of the board of visitors oversees all committee functions and reports annually to the appropriate trustee committee at that committee's on-campus annual retreat. The written report is responded to by the university administration, and the board of trustees reviews both the report and the response.

EXHIBIT 3.3

This practice contrasts with the way another board selected trustees: "It was done by a few insiders who would invite their friends to come on the board, regardless of their qualifications. The votes were just too personal. In effect, you had to vote for the candidates or against the nominator."

"Chemistry"

All boards seek capable people to serve as trustees; however, the best boards value the ability of individuals to work within a group even more highly than professional skills and career accomplishments. Boards rarely falter from lack of expertise in law, business, real estate, and other areas that tend to be emphasized in profiles of the ideal composition of a board. "What do we expect of trustees?" asked a trustee of an able board. "We expect good attendance and other things like that. It's all in writing. I guess what's not in writing is the value we place on collegiality. There have been particularly bright, successful individuals we've not asked to be on the board because the chemistry wasn't right."

In the search for new college trustees, too few boards pay much attention to whether candidates have experience with complex organizations and with the consensus-driven decision-making processes that typify governance at most academic institutions. An entrepreneur whose success was due to swift and autonomous decision making may have little tolerance for board deliberations, much less constituent consultation. While independent go-getters may appear attractive at first blush, these very same traits can be disruptive to a board's harmony.

Similarly, while boards may weigh factors such as gender, age, race, and occupational background, not many recognize the need to have a balance of listeners and talkers, short-term and long-term thinkers, task-oriented and process-oriented people, and iconoclasts and consensus builders. One extraordinarily capable board had trustee positions tacitly reserved for "different drummers." This unusually congenial board worried that its sociability could inhibit complex thinking. Thus, the trusteeship committee set out to find individuals who might challenge the group's assumptions. At the same time, the different drummers could not be too brash or aggressive because such behavior would violate the board's norm of rational discourse. In the estimation of most trustees, the best different drummer appointed to the board was an erudite trial attorney who genuinely loved the institution and admired the board but whose greatest enjoyment came from a good debate. In the absence of respect for the institution and the board, this trustee's argumentativeness would have been counterproductive.

In the same vein, a member of another board made clear that good chemistry does not and should not mean total agreement on every issue.

> We're not afraid of confrontation. We want intelligent and thoughtful participation. If you don't speak up, you won't last. If you have concerns,

put them on the table, and leave them on the table when you leave the room. This board expects everyone to be friends—not just cordial, but friends. We like each other, and that's important. I think it's part of being midwestern. There's less ego, and people really believe in teamwork.

Orientation

Effective boards view orientation as an essential step to incorporate new trustees into the group quickly. Chapter 4 considers the substantive elements of orientation to the *institution*; here, we describe orientation to *trusteeship* and *the board*.

The majority of boards overlook an "internal" orientation to the board in favor of reviewing the college's organizational chart, strategic plan, and balance sheet, and touring the facilities. Yet, the functioning of the board and the role trustees play are the aspects of the position least likely to be familiar to new board members, even those who have been trustees elsewhere. Each board has its own history, traditions, culture, and chemistry; a key goal of an orientation should be to make these "unwritten rules" as explicit as possible. The program should answer questions most prospective trustees would not even think to ask. Is it a violation of group norms to miss meetings, to arrive late, or to leave early? What should I do if I disagree (maybe strenuously) with the president, a senior staff member, a board committee, or the leadership of the board? What do I do with grapevine information from faculty or students? How should I handle calls from the press or from elected public officials? Can I contact senior staff directly, or should I go through the president? Are there any taboo topics? Any cliques within the board? How does the board feel about trustees doing business with the institution, even if the conflict-of-interest guidelines are heeded? The easiest way to decide what to cover is to ask present trustees one question: "What do you know now that you wish you had known when you joined the board?" If newcomers are provided with that information at the outset, most will feel comfortable much sooner as members of the group. In other words, orientation should: (1) help new members understand the board's norms and preferred protocol of behavior; (2) explain how the board *really* works; and (3) illustrate, by the very nature of the program, that there are no secrets or forbidden questions.

In contrast, when orientations duck significant issues, problems can ensue. On one college's board, for instance, some trustees believe that they have an entitlement, in effect, to certain student admissions slots, or at least to great sway over "special" cases. Other trustees painfully avoid advocacy for any candidates. If and when this board learns, as the president already knows, that some trustees presume to wield great influence while others believe that individual admission decisions should be beyond the board's purview, rifts within the board are likely to widen. The source of the problem is that the trustees have failed to delineate at orientation or elsewhere mutual expectations and explicit "rules of the game."

Installation Ceremonies

Colleges and universities are replete with ceremonies designed to welcome and educate new students (freshman orientation), to inform and inspire (convocation), to celebrate academic achievement (graduation), and to commemorate new leadership (presidential inauguration)—to say nothing of the thrill and inspiration of athletic events! Other nonprofits mark performances, openings, and other institutional accomplishments with formal celebrations. It is especially appropriate in institutions that derive so much meaning from ceremony that a board adopt rituals to convey the meaning of trusteeship and to welcome new trustees into the stream of institutional history.

Some college boards have developed installation ceremonies and other traditions to welcome new trustees and to symbolize the significance and equality of membership in the group. At one college, the board asks each new member to respond formally to the commitment questions included in Exhibit 3.4. The new trustee is then introduced to the board by his or her "mentor" (see next section).

A Trustee Installation Ceremony

Trustees elected to office stand before the chair of the board, who says:

"You have been duly elected trustees of this college. Your office is consecrated by its importance to the college's welfare. You will always bear in mind that what you do will in high degree determine the college's future. You will look upon your office as an opportunity to serve others.

"Your office being thus acknowledged, you are asked to express your purpose regarding it by answering 'I do' to the following questions:

1. Do you promise to lead this college toward the achievement of the high educational, ethical, and spiritual goals that have been its objectives from the beginning?
2. Do you promise to serve in every way possible to promote the cause of higher education through this college?
3. Do you promise to give diligent service to the affairs of this college?

"I now welcome you to the office of trustee of this college, and to the fellowship of the board."

EXHIBIT 3.4

At another college, the board asks each newcomer to present orally a brief autobiography, with special emphasis on personal interests and previous service to the institution. The new trustee then signs a book that includes the names of all trustees who have served on the board since the institution was founded. Another board developed an unusual initiation "rite": the price of admission to the board includes telling one clean joke over dinner that gets a laugh. Newcomers know about this beloved custom in advance, so no one is surprised or embarrassed. While the technique would not work for every board, it illustrates the power of a special tradition to bind a group together.

Mentors

Many effective boards extend the impact of orientation by appointing a mentor or coach, an experienced board member, to guide the new trustee during his or her first year in office (see Exhibit 3.5). The practice sends a strong message to new trustees: "We want you to feel welcome. We want you to learn what you need to know in order to become, as quickly as possible, a fully contributing member of the group." Mentors are particularly helpful to

---

The Mentor System for New Trustees

What is the mentor system? It is a practice whereby each new member of the board of trustees is paired with an experienced trustee who serves as a mentor during the new member's first year on the board.

Why does the college use the mentor system? The mentor system is one way to help welcome and orient new members and to incorporate them into the fabric and work of the board of trustees. It accelerates the process by which new trustees come to be comfortable and effective members of the board.

Who makes the "match" between the mentor and the new trustee? It is done by the Committee on Trusteeship, which invites experienced trustees to serve as mentors to newcomers on the board.

What criteria are used? The committee tries to choose a mentor who has a prior acquaintance with the new board member and/or common interests.

What is expected of a mentor?

- Phone or, if at all possible, visit the new trustee to extend a welcome prior to his or her first board meeting. During this initial conversation, the mentor should provide an overview of the upcoming orientation, and answer any questions the new trustee may have.
- Attend the Thursday evening portion of the orientation program and introduce the newcomer to other members of the board and the staff. (The orientation will continue on Friday. If there is no organized orientation program at the time of the newcomer's first meeting, the mentor should invite the new trustee to attend committee meetings with him or her.)
- Whenever possible, sit next to the new trustee during board and committee meetings to answer any questions that may arise, to provide any background briefings, or to direct the newcomer to an appropriate source of information or expertise.
- Phone the new trustee at least once between board meetings during the first year, just to touch base and to offer assistance.
- Encourage phone calls from the newcomer at any other time that he or she may have a question, a concern, or a need for advice.

EXHIBIT 3.5

unravel the intricacies of institutional history and to interpret the organizational culture to a new trustee. "Occasionally, people in the know—maybe including me—talk in shorthand, and it gets in the way of cohesiveness because it leaves out the people who are less experienced on the board." A typical approach was described by a newer trustee of one college:

> Your mentor sits next to you at meetings and steers you through agendas and procedures. There are a lot of little things you have to learn, about parliamentary procedure and that sort of thing, but also about the institution and the board. With a mentor, there is someone there for questions as you need to ask them. It also is the responsibility of the mentor to introduce you to others on the board. They get you around, and you get to know people more quickly.

The chair of this board said:

> We pick mentors from both on and off the committee on trusteeship. We think about ages and interests. We try to get the mentors to attend the orientation with the new trustee. Basically, we put our arms around them for the first couple of meetings. We want to get them up to speed as quickly as possible.

THE TRUSTEESHIP COMMITTEE'S ROLE IN BUILDING BOARD COHESIVENESS

A trusteeship committee serves as a champion for the board's effectiveness and well-being, much as an academic affairs committee aspires to ensure a top-drawer educational program, or a finance committee endeavors to safeguard an institution's financial stability. Without a committee responsible for the board's welfare, questions of cohesiveness and effectiveness will likely be lost in the press of other activities and priorities. "Having a group of people who think about the contributions each individual trustee can make, who think carefully about committee assignments, and who plan for leadership succession is very useful," noted a member of a committee on trusteeship.

To have real impact, the committee should have an expanded charge and influential members. "We just broadened the committee's role beyond just getting skilled people on the board," related a board chairman. "The committee nominates trustees and board officers and is responsible for the orientation, continuing education, and criteria for the evaluation of board members." Whereas some boards are tempted to pack the committee with "sensitive" types or with trustees from the "helping professions," the committee, in fact, should include the president and the board chair along with other experienced and respected trustees.

While a trusteeship committee should be concerned with the performance of individual trustees as well as the board as a whole, most tend, understandably, to be ill at ease with assessments of individual board members. Typical of most trustees' experience, a board member allowed, "I don't think I've ever heard anyone say anything in a formal capacity at a board meeting about individual performance. Occasionally an individual will leave because of nonattendance, but that's about it."

How can trustee assessment be used to unite rather than divide a board? One board chair responded:

> It could be a marvelous tool to have a trustee self-evaluate. It is impossible for a variety of reasons to tell a trustee, "You're not performing up to expectations." Maybe they're large donors or are experiencing personal difficulties, and you certainly don't want to alienate anyone. But if they had some sort of real one-on-one, either with the president or the chair of the trusteeship committee, then I think they would be able to honestly assess their own performance against their own goals. And at the end of the session they could be asked, "Do you really feel that you can continue to serve?" Because you really can't kick someone off, you can't even not reelect them to a second term. But a meeting like that might provide more opportunities for change.

In reality, boards have realized that such conversations can give an underperformer the necessary "out" to leave the board voluntarily or to open a discussion about why the individual has been so disengaged and what can be done to ameliorate the situation.

With respect to what can be done, the trusteeship committee's ability to encourage a cohesive board demands a mindset that places considerable responsibility on the shoulders of the board itself to make trustees effective. Involvement and influence on the board are not viewed as prizes to be won by those willing to fight aggressively for them. Competent boards assume an affirmative obligation to involve individuals in the work of governance, and they regard poor performance by trustees as attributable just as much or more to board failure than to personal ineptitude.

> The board affairs committee has private conversations about members who are falling by the way, trying to figure out how to engage them.

> The leadership of the board has become more conscientious about trustee assignments and opportunities for service. They really look at how each trustee can become more engaged in the life of the institution.

Renegade trustees, also known as "loose cannons" and "cowboys," should be treated differently from underperformers. These individuals repeatedly breach the board's norms; for example, by violating confidences, behaving boorishly, instigating cliques, attempting to exercise undue influence, or acting on behalf of the institution without authorization. Normally, the board chair should confront and counsel the renegade, one-on-one. Certainly, the institution's CEO, however tempted to do so, should not. Board discipline is *not* the president's province, even by default. The risks are too high and the stakes are too great to engage the CEO on this front. In egregious cases, the committee on trusteeship might meet with the individual to emphasize that his or actions affront not just the chair or the CEO, but the entire board. If these interventions fail, the trusteeship committee often responds through nonrenewal at the end of the trustee's term.

LEADERSHIP

When we asked trustees from the Trustee Demonstration Project sites, "What advice would you offer to another board about how to improve?" the preponderance of responses emphasized the role of leadership. "Start at the top. Are your president and board chair capable, skilled, and committed to improvement? If not, make change there first." "You'd better have good leadership. There's no substitute for it." Without the active support of the president and the chair, boards may still be able to function cohesively; however, the odds are not very favorable.

The Role of the Institution's President

A board chair cautioned, "You can't improve a board without an excellent rapport between the board and the [institution's] president. If the president is uncomfortable and uneasy, it won't happen, it won't work." Many of the suggestions in this chapter for enhancing group cohesion depend directly and obviously on the commitment of the institution's president or CEO; for example, whether the president communicates narrowly to influential members or broadly to the entire board, whether agendas and arrangements for board meetings facilitate or hinder participation, and whether social events are organized that enable trustees to become better acquainted. "It's hard for a board to pull itself up by its own bootstraps."

Unfortunately, the presidents of some institutions work harder to cement trustee loyalty to themselves than to the board. "Some people are on the board because they like the president. If he left, they would look hard at whether they want to devote as much time to the university." That president has built a board of corporate executives and entrepreneurs who devalue teamwork and derive satisfaction primarily from individual relationships with the president and from individual efforts on behalf of the institution.

Other CEOs undercut cohesiveness by inhibiting or denigrating individual trustees. If the institution's president does not treat *all* trustees respectfully (and, more to the point, if the board does not insist on that), then the sense of the board as a group can be shattered because the president, and not the board, defines the norms and the terms of "legitimate" membership.

In one instance, a board member questioned the assumptions underlying the budget and, as a bystander trustee recounted, "the president upbraided him, telling him it wasn't his place to raise a question. He had great common sense and the will to challenge, but I'm not sure after being shot down like that he'll raise a question again." In some cases, such an attack could unite a board, albeit in opposition to the president. In this situation, where trustees were relatively uninformed about institutional issues and unsure of their role, the "attack," as it came to be known, further weakened the board's collective confidence, increased individual dependence on the president, and left some trustees chary about raising questions and confronting the president or the institution's problems. On the other hand, the chair-elect scored this one "a *near*-term victory for the president," implying that such intimidating tactics by the CEO would not be tolerated in the future.

The Role of the Board Chair

"How do you improve a board's performance? Get a smart chair." Among members of effective boards, the definition of "smart" connotes the chair's ability to encourage board cohesion and inclusiveness and to attend to group process.

> Sometimes when we don't know what to do about something, we're just bouncing off the walls. That's where our chair is so good. He just allows us to bounce and get all the diverse ideas on the table. Then he plots out what he thinks he has heard. He doesn't try to tell us the answer but helps to structure the discussion to develop a common consensus.

Unfortunately, not all chairs are so gifted, and not all boards are so blessed. Many preside without leading; that is, without doing much to enhance the ability of trustees to function as a board. "Our former chair would come to board meetings without preparation, having thought about the issues for only a few minutes before."

Most opportunities for the chair to stimulate or stifle the development of the board as a team occur, of course, during meetings. In that venue, some chairs have learned the language of inclusiveness and group process without absorbing the lessons. "We meet from 8:30 in the morning to 1:00 in the afternoon. Although discussion is supposed to be welcome, the chairman is very soon looking at his watch if we fall behind schedule. If you have anything you want to ask or say, you really feel like you are risking having the meeting run into lunch time." At another institution with a time-conscious chair, the board agreed at a recent retreat to hold an executive session at the end of each board meeting. At the very next meeting, the chair abruptly called for adjournment with a proviso that the board could reconvene in executive session if anyone so requested. Needless to say, no one did.

An astute chair, by contrast, does not confuse efficiency with effectiveness, or assume that a board can coalesce "on the fly." "Some people are now saying, 'Let's be more organized and make the meetings shorter.' I feel we can't meet that schedule if it means cutting off meaningful debate of issues. I don't want an agenda so tight that it limits the time we need." Furthermore, effective chairs are sensitive to the importance of inclusiveness as the "glue" that holds the board together. "It's a main responsibility of a chair to say, 'I haven't heard from you all day,' or 'How do you see this?'" "If someone brought up a topic and there was no discussion, I would know something was amiss. Part of it is just sensing. Is everyone getting along all right? Does anyone feel left out?"

Other chairs fail to attend to group process or to patrol the boundaries of acceptable trustee behavior outside the boardroom. As a faction of one college board lobbied to dismiss the president, and the "clique got noisier and noisier, the chair didn't exercise control over them and eventually allowed them to undermine an orderly process for dealing with the problem. The group damaged the board inside and outside, and the chair let it happen." Instances like this leave the team-oriented trustees dispirited and the "cowboys" poised to fill the leadership void.

Leadership Succession

The failure to prepare trustees for positions of leadership afflicts most boards. Many trustees, and occasionally some board chairs, do not understand how leadership decisions are made. "It's a process of osmosis. You get on a committee, and then you're made chair. You don't really know why—maybe because you've impressed the right people. It's not like it's done in a business. There aren't any obvious stepping stones." This circumstance leaves many CEOs and trustees anxious about the future of the board as a unified entity.

Effective boards groom leaders because the failure to do so produces excessive dependence on a few trustees (too often retirees or people "in transition") and raises the specter of an empty cupboard when the board needs new leaders. Without attention to leadership succession, chairs frequently remain in office too long—often 10 or more years, rather than 4 or 5, the norm among effective boards. Lack of turnover concentrates too much power in the same hands and reinforces the corrosive idea that the board lacks depth of leadership. For obvious reasons, this weakens the board's sense of collective capability and makes it difficult for trustees to think of themselves as part of a stable, ongoing group.

Because leadership is so essential, competent boards accord special attention to nurturing future officers. No responsible corporate executive would fail to groom new leaders, even one's successor. Board officers should be equally conscientious. "When the previous chair took office, he was the only logical choice. Now there are five or six. We've enlarged the executive committee, put people in ad hoc leadership positions, put them on the presidential search committee, and just reached out to more people."

The trusteeship committee should systematically assess the pool of potential leaders and then provide assignments, committee rotations, and educational opportunities to ready these individuals for greater responsibility. Some boards also name a chair elect to learn at the current chair's side. "We have taken the step of appointing a chair elect soon after the new chair takes office, thus giving him some help and the successor some time to study and learn the role."

Even when a board attends to leadership development, trustees will still face the need, from time to time, to actually select leaders, particularly a chair. The irony is that the better the board has done in selecting trustees and developing leadership skills, the *more* difficult the choices will be. Unlike the typical board that would be fortunate to have one able person available to serve as chair, a board that has been attentive to leadership development may have several reasonable prospects.

In choosing a board chair, trustees and CEOs worry simultaneously about two problems. The first is that, to protect the feelings of those considered but not selected, an in-group will choose the chair and run the risk that the rest of the board will resent being excluded from the process, and second, that a completely open process will lead to embarrassment as one candidate wins and others lose. In an effort to allay both of these concerns, one board asked two consultants to help the trustees revamp the board chair selection process at a retreat. The process worked successfully there and at several other institutions thereafter.

First, at the retreat, the entire board discussed these questions:

- What are the responsibilities of the board chair?
- How will you know when the job is performed well?
- What personal and professional attributes and competencies should the board chair have?

After the retreat, the trusteeship committee circulated to all trustees a list of the board's responses. A few days later, members of the committee called each trustee to seek nominees, in light of the conclusions from the retreat discussion.

Once all the calls were completed, the committee met to compare notes. Two trustees appeared to have approximately equal support for the office, although everyone had positive feelings about both individuals. The committee chair called both trustees to tell them that their names had surfaced and to inquire if they would be willing to serve as chair if asked. Both responded affirmatively. In a second round of calls, committee members asked trustees to react to the top contenders. With just two names to consider, one of the two emerged as preferable. The committee chair called both individuals again: to ask one to stand for election and to tell the other that he had very strong support, but that the trustees gave a slight edge to the other individual because of her more extensive fundraising experience. The goal of the process—to bring a single, qualified nominee to the board for election—was accomplished.

The procedure gave every trustee an opportunity to reflect on the nature of the chair's role and to contribute to the list of requirements. The process also reinforced the fact that not everyone is prepared to fulfill the chair's role effectively. Third, the entire board was involved in selecting its leadership, and no inside group functioned as a "king maker." Finally, the process avoided the embarrassment that would have come with a public election in which there would have been a winner and one or more losers. Regardless of the specifics, the selection process should, like this one, be known to the full board, provide all trustees with the opportunity to influence the selection criteria, and allow everyone a chance to voice an opinion and eventually to cast a vote. A team can not afford to leave the selection of its "captain" to chance.

CONCLUSION

In many ways, boards of trustees are peculiar bodies: groups of part-time amateurs responsible for governing often highly specialized and professionally sophisticated multimillion-dollar enterprises replete with full-time experts. Small wonder that the institution's administrators and even the trustees themselves sometimes wonder about the wisdom and viability of the concept.

Nevertheless, a collection of able individuals who learn to operate as a cohesive and goal-oriented entity can be a formidable source of strength for an institution: a bulwark for the president; a source of ideas, insights, and solutions; and a powerful advocate in the community. What distinguishes this kind of board from a fragmented collection of individuals with separate agendas is rarely intellectual capacity or professional expertise. Rather, the differences are embedded in what boards *do* with the trustee commitment and talent they have. The most competent boards consciously form and assiduously maintain a cohesive unit, in which the whole is more than the sum of the parts.

CHAPTER

········

Getting Smart:
The Key to Governing
Smart

THE NEED TO KNOW

In "Empowering the Board" (1995), Harvard Business School professor Jay Lorsch observes that the two most important sources of power for corporate boards are knowledge and cohesion. Lorsch carefully distinguishes between information, or operational data, and knowledge, the acquired intelligence necessary to understand and interpret an organization's context, culture, strategy, markets, technology, and relative performance.

In "The Promise of the Governed Corporation" (1995), another Harvard professor, John Pound, posits that, above all else, "board members must be expert. Directors must be well versed in the complexities of the company and its industry, of finance and financial structure, and of relevant law and regulation." Directors must attain a threshold of expertise "sufficient to allow the board to add value to the decision-making process" (93–94).

Despite the powerful connection between knowledge or expertise and effectiveness, remarkably few corporate or nonprofit boards make a concerted effort to acquire the scope of knowledge essential to govern intelligently. Indicative of this oversight, some 150 nonprofit boards scored, on average, lowest on the educational dimension of trusteeship, as measured by self-assessment surveys of board competence (see Exhibit 1.1). The educational dimension concerns whether "the board takes the necessary steps to ensure that trustees are knowledgeable about the institution, the profession, and the board's roles, responsibilities, and performance" (Chait, Holland, and Taylor 1991, 2). On a scale from 0 to 1, the mean score on the educational dimension was .42, whereas the mean for the other five dimensions combined was .72, almost 60% higher.

On the one hand, these numbers are a cause for concern: most boards do not consciously and systematically create opportunities to expand the knowledge base of trustees. On the other hand, boards that participated in the Trustee Demonstration Project did improve markedly on the educational dimension. At the start of the project, the sites' average score was .43; four years later the average score had risen to .60, a 72% increase. These numbers from self-assessments were corroborated by a 66% increase in the educational dimension scores drawn from interviews with trustees before and after the project. In other words, trustees, when coached, can learn how to learn.

While always important, the ability to learn has assumed heightened significance since 1990 when Peter Senge introduced the concept of "'learning organizations,' organizations where people continually expand their capacity to create the results they truly desire, where new and expansive patterns of thinking are nurtured, where collective aspiration is set free, and where people are continually learning how to learn together" (1990, 1). In an ever more competitive environment, scholars and managers alike recognize that comparative advantage stems not so much from accumulated intellectual capital as from the capacity to generate new knowledge and the wherewithal to modify organizational behavior "to reflect new knowledge and insights. . . . Without accompanying changes in the way that work gets done, only the potential for improvement exists" (Garvin 1993, 80). In fact, the concept of the learning organization has become so popular that many corporations such as Coca-Cola, Hewlett-Packard, and Monsanto have actually established the executive level position of chief learning officer or chief knowledge officer (Ward 1996).

THE RELUCTANCE TO LEARN

Above all else, a "learning organization" means that the institution's leaders, namely the board and senior management, have ample opportunities and a strong appetite to acquire knowledge. If steady opportunities to learn are so crucial to the effective governance and successful performance of corporations, then why do most nonprofit boards neglect trustee education? The answer rests partially on the presumption, often by both the board and the staff, that trustees are already well-versed and knowledgeable. Board members are, almost by definition, bright people who understand how the world works. "The better trustees are very successful people. They assume they know whatever it is they need to know to be good members. They don't think they need help," explained a college president. Therefore, trustees usually assume the roles of counselors, advisers, and teachers rather than the roles of students and learners. Board members are primarily considered a source of knowledge—not individuals with a need for knowledge.

Whatever specific intelligence trustees may lack about the nature of the institution or the profession, many board members believe that years of successful experience in the for-profit sector and a first-hand acquaintance with the institution, for example, as a student, parent, patron, or beneficiary, more than offset any knowledge deficit. School and college trustees have argued, "I attended college. I attended *this* college. I have children at this college. What more do I need to know?"

Were the situation reversed, trustees would quickly see the folly of this argument. Imagine that a particularly able university president were appointed to the board of directors of an airline. As a long-time, competent executive of a complex nonprofit entity and as a frequent flier, this president might see little need to learn more about the nature of the airline or the economics of the industry. How different could it be? In fact, the odds are that the university president would already assume that he or she knew the strategic priorities of the company: more legroom and better meals in coach class (as opposed to challenges from subsidized foreign carriers and nonunionized domestic airlines, for example). And the president's prior experience would suggest that changes of policy or strategy should be implemented through a highly consultative, consensus-oriented process with the flight attendants and the kitchen crews, rather than through an analysis by senior management. Trustees of nonprofits are subject to the very same errors.

To compound the problem, both trustees and staff unintentionally conspire to suppress recognition and discussion of the board's knowledge gaps. From the trustees' perspective, many are reluctant to admit to any ignorance for fear of being embarrassed or exposed as perhaps not as erudite as everyone may have assumed. Thus, we have watched college board members, for example, struggle with fund accounts, puzzle over the promotion and tenure process, or pretend to understand the concept of shared governance. Some may ask to be enlightened privately; most simply leave baffled.

Senior staff are equally hesitant to highlight the board's knowledge deficits. In some cases, executives are understandably loath to suggest or impose "remedial education" for such accomplished individuals. In other cases, staff worry that an informed board could be downright dangerous and dysfunctional. A board that knows "too much" may interfere in the operations of the institution, intrude on professional prerogatives, and strain constituent relations. As one CEO commented, "far better to keep the board at bay."

Even in situations where the board and the CEO may be more positively disposed to trustee education, other impediments arise. Most notably, staff and trustees lack, respectively, the time to develop and the time to attend education sessions. Boards and trustee committees are already too overscheduled to permit any "interludes" for education. The urgent drives out the important; the imperative to act displaces the need to learn.

THE PRICE OF IGNORANCE

In response to concerns about the allegedly exorbitant costs of a college education, Derek Bok, then president of Harvard University, replied, "If you think education is expensive, try ignorance." The same could be said about corporate and nonprofit governance.

Without sufficient knowledge about the economy, the industry, the company, and relevant technologies, corporate directors cannot govern successfully. As the director of a failed bank commented:

> Any board member who is not committed to educating himself about the business of his board should resign. . . . [A director] must make the time to learn about the business on which board he sits. Directors must come to grips with the fundamental fact that it is impossible to understand the operations of a company—and therefore to be an effective director— merely attending regularly called board meetings. (Jacobs 1991)

This admonition applies to the trustees of nonprofits, as well. How can a board govern when the trustees lack a fundamental understanding of the institution's profession, context, and organizational culture? The short answer is, "not well." The most obvious consequences of the board's ignorance are: (1) an overreliance on the professional staff to develop policies, formulate strategies, and evaluate implications; (2) an inability to independently monitor and interpret results; and (3) a limitation on the board's sphere of concern to financial and related fiduciary responsibilities, to the exclusion of policy and strategy decisions in other domains. No board can responsibly afford to pay such a high price.

By the same token, trustees determined to become well informed confront a stiff challenge: the knowledge gaps are wide and difficult to overcome. Within the for-profit sector, at least the basic "rules of the game" to succeed as a business are familiar to board members, irrespective of the particular industry. By contrast, trustees of nonprofits typically enter a foreign culture with curious customs and unusual axioms. To cite only a few examples from higher education: some "successes" lose money; competition often drives prices up, not down; senior managers frequently have less power than tenured professors; and "swiftly" may mean within a year or two. Even more formidable are the obstacles to understand the quality of the institution's core products: instruction, research, and service. There are few measures that are widely accepted by professionals and easily grasped by lay persons. We do not mean to imply that trustees must accept these circumstances as immutable. Rather, we would submit that boards eager to encourage the academy to adopt new ways would do well to first grasp the old ways. In short, trustees have much to learn.

RESPONSIBILITY FOR TRUSTEE EDUCATION

Effective boards are not self-educated about academe or about governance. Instead, better boards acknowledge the need to learn, identify topics to explore, direct the administration to arrange appropriate programs, and encourage trustees to participate. As a constructive first step, the trustees can assign overall coordination for board education to the committee on trusteeship or a comparable committee. This committee would be expected to champion the importance of trustee education and to monitor and fulfill (with the staff) the board's educational needs. Specific steps are described later in this chapter.

Beyond that elementary step, the board should include the president's effectiveness as a trustee educator as an element of the CEO's annual performance review. Did the president (and the senior staff) systematically enhance the board's knowledge of the institution and the profession and respond to trustee requests to become better informed?

To a significant degree, senior management bears the burden of implementation for trustee education. As professionals, the staff are apt to recognize weaknesses in the board's knowledge base. In response, management might then, at a minimum, distribute articles to read, suggest conferences to attend, or recommend experts to address the board. More importantly, the staff's responsibility for trustee education will be discharged though the materials provided to board members and through the discussions the staff facilitates (see Chapter 6).

Unfortunately, some executives bury board members under an avalanche of *information*. By contrast, enlightened presidents identify and communicate to trustees the specific *knowledge* necessary to comprehend the college's context and to discuss intelligently questions of policy and strategy. To return to the distinction drawn by Jay Lorsch at the beginning of this chapter:

> *Knowledge* is the more appropriate word here instead of the more frequently used *information* because the directors' real problem is not lack of information but its content and context . . . [B]oards spend too much time watching presentations when what they really need is to understand the material presented so they can participate more effectively. . . . The challenge for directors is to take what may be a greater quantity and broader array of information and turn it into useful knowledge quickly. (Lorsch 1995, 116)

Some management teams do create occasions for trustees to absorb essential information, for example, about the competitive environment, the quality of products and services, organizational culture, and critical performance indicators. Far more typically, management does not furnish the strategic context and analytical interpretations that convert such information into knowledge—the intelligence that enables college trustees, for example, to draw policy and strategy implications from indicators of institutional performance such as financial aid packages, admissions yields, student evaluations of instruction, investments in technology, endowment performance, or some other strategic indicator.

Only a small minority of CEOs deliberately and deviously withhold such material. The usual explanations for these omissions are that trustees lack the time, desire, or aptitude to be educated, and that complicated and subtle matters—not easily grasped by lay persons—best remain within the orbit of the faculty and the staff. These "excuses" are, as one president declared, self-destructive.

> Any president who doesn't see that a well-informed board is not a benefit is being extraordinarily short-sighted. Even if you are being selfishly pragmatic, you might be able to fend off and hold the board at arm's length for a short period of time, but eventually something will happen that will upset them. And they won't have the context to understand the institution or your leadership style, and then you are playing with dynamite because you're going to get blown out.

To summarize, the trustees and senior management must be mutually dedicated to the development of a knowledgeable board.

The board must establish a climate that stresses the need for trustees to be knowledgeable and that encourages trustees to disclose knowledge deficits. Then, the board and staff together must create attractive and accessible opportunities for trustees to tie information and education to strategy and context so as to produce an enlightened board. Unfortunately and ironically, even many *educational* institutions fail to do so.

WAYS TO LEARN

Among the questions we asked scores of trustees over the course of the project was, "How did you learn to be an effective board member?" The answers were remarkably similar, as illustrated by a representative sample of responses.

> When I came on the board, there was nothing formal in the way of education. I just met the others and went to work, learning as I went along.

> Nothing. No one gave me any instruction, expectations, or guidance whatever.

> The main education is on-the-job training, osmosis. You learn by attending and participating.

> By watching and listening . . . through observation and experience on other boards.

Other than the session for newcomers, there isn't much education about what you do on the board. . . . I'm not sure that people understand what they're supposed to do at board meetings except listen.

I watch the leaders and see what they are trying to do and how they go about it.

I talk to a friend on the board.

These comments reveal certain common themes. First, the education of trustees tends to be either nonexistent or utterly casual and haphazard. There are few methodical, intentional efforts to educate board members, an omission that slows the trustees' "learning curve" and limits the board's potential. Second, most trustees have little choice except to learn passively, most often through observation, even as colleges and schools increasingly recognize the superior power of active learning. Third, the absence of trustee education programs implicitly conveys an indifference to the value of education more generally, a strange message to emit from the boardrooms of colleges (as well as schools, museums, libraries, and hospitals) where teaching and learning are central to the organization's mission. If boards are to exercise responsible, knowledgeable leadership, and if boards are to reflect the college's commitment to learning, then clearly changes in the rather pitiful "state of the art" of trustee education are in order.

All colleges and universities offer numerous modes for student learning: formal classes, residential programs, library searches, computer-based instruction, and student organizations. Furthermore, an effective education encompasses a variety of pedagogies, each matched to the nature of the material, the learning objectives, and student and faculty preferences. Trustee education should exhibit the same characteristics: multiple occasions to learn and instructional approaches appropriate to the topic and the audience. Fortunately, as the experiences of the Trustee Demonstration Project sites illustrated, these are attainable goals.

Orientation Programs

These represent the "core curriculum" or general education component of a board's edification. (Chapter 2 addresses orientation to trusteeship *per se*.) Here, trustees acquire the basic *knowledge* every board member should possess, such as the mission and history of the institution, the hallmarks of the organization's culture (especially as contrasted with corporate culture), the nature of the competitive environment, the institution's comparative advantages, the sources and uses of funds, the distribution of power and authority, and the dynamics and economics of institutional productivity. Unfortunately, many orientation programs are consumed by comparatively less important information such as a detailed review of the board's bylaws, an extensive tour of the physical plant, or a lengthy elaboration of the organization chart.

How can a committee on trusteeship discover what new trustees truly need to know? Ask past and present trustees. The design of a trustee orientation program could begin with a one-question survey of current and former trustees: "What do you know now that you wish you had known when you first joined the board?" The answers to this question should constitute a significant component of the curriculum to acquaint new trustees with the institution. With a "syllabus" organized around these responses, orientation programs will provide relevant material and shorten the "start-up" phase for neophytes on the board. As one institution's CEO noted about an orientation so replete with knowledge that even experienced trustees regularly attended the program, "the orientation provided the equivalent of a year's worth of service for new trustees."

While current and former board members are particularly well equipped to recommend what newcomers need to know, the self-declared information needs of new trustees should not be overlooked. If asked, new board members will cite areas where a "crash course" would be helpful. When actually offered the chance to identify knowledge gaps, newcomers to college and university boards have requested, for example, a tutorial in fund accounting, an invitation to shadow a professor for a day or two, and an introduction to the performance metrics or yardsticks used to assess a university's competitive position.

Although some aspects of orientation—and trustee education more generally—should be conducted face to face, other segments might be provided by audiotapes, videotapes, or even in electronic format, accessible by computer. Once developed, such resources dramatically reduce the need to start afresh with each orientation program.

Finally, boards should realize that orientation programs need not be only for new trustees. Two boards in the demonstration project expect *all* trustees to attend the orientation (and most do), both as a way to welcome newcomers and as a way to be to updated and "re-educated." Several other boards tap current and even former trustees to present portions of the orientation program—another nice touch to acquaint trustees with one another and to instill a sense of community and continuity within the board.

Ongoing Trustee Education

Trustee education cannot be confined to the orientation program. Instead, there must be a continuous process that offers advanced knowledge for the entire board and specialized knowledge for various trustee committees. Educational efforts for the whole board must be germane to the institutional strategy and the board's concerns. If the content misses the mark—no matter how clever the format—the value of the instruction and trustee enthusiasm for the process will plummet.

How can relevancy be assured? As with orientations, "Just ask." Senior staff and trustees in leadership positions should periodically poll the entire board to elicit topics and issues on which veteran trustees may wish to accumulate more intellectual capital. One college's board asks all trustees, as part of an annual self-evaluation, "What do you need to know in order to be a more valuable member of this board?" A typical response: "We need to be better educated about the institution's finances, student performance, the environment of the university, and academic quality indicators." Other institutions incorporate into an evaluation form, completed after each board meeting, questions about whether the trustees lacked vital knowledge or information to address the issues at hand.

The board of an independent school adopted a still more inventive approach: a "pop quiz" that asked trustees 30 factual questions about the school. The quizzes were self-administered and the results were private. Questions addressed enrollments, gender balance, curriculum requirements, faculty award winners, the value of the endowment, the median faculty salary, and the number of staff. The purpose of the exercise was to help trustees assess their knowledge of the school and to gently prod individuals with low scores to request programs and activities to become better informed.

Whatever the particular techniques, once the board's educational needs are clarified and connected to strategic priorities, the institution can design appropriate responses. Based on the experiences of the project sites, we offer seven options that can be employed separately or together. The first three are largely internal to the board; the final four cases are opportunities for the board to learn from other sources.

Mini-seminars

Mini-seminars are presentation and discussion sessions organized around a special topic. The issues are normally determined by the trustees, either through a poll, at the suggestion of the president, or by the committee on trusteeship. Most are one- or two-hour modules of a regular board meeting; some include remarks by an outside expert. When asked to identify the most important change made by the board in the last three years, the chair of an especially effective board answered:

> We do a better job of educating members about the board and about the institution. We have consciously structured sessions at the board meetings where we specifically try to educate. We have instituted an educational segment at just about every board meeting, and recently those have been given by the academic departments. The purpose of these segments is both to learn more about the academic programs and also more about other members of our community.

At one college, where the board's scores on the educational dimension nearly doubled, the trustees charged the committee on trusteeship to schedule an "education hour" at every board meeting, focused on a key question before one of the trustees' four policy committees. The seminars included

- a program on the operation and philosophy of faculty governance, with a panel of faculty senate leaders and one faculty critic of the current system
- a lecture by a national authority on the college presidency on leadership transitions and the role boards should play to smooth the entry of a new CEO
- a discussion, guided by experts on the board, of endowment management

The commitment to ongoing trustee education "will continue," the chair of the trusteeship committee maintained, because "everyone realizes its importance." Another site with a less dramatic (though still substantial) increase in the educational dimension had, among a series of hour-long sessions, one on fund accounting—provided gratis by the college's auditors—and another with a national expert on the future of the denomination's college. A third institution organized a seminar around admissions, with presentations by the dean of enrollment management and a talk by the president of the state's association for independent colleges. As a result, one trustee noted, "We have a fresh sense of key trends in the external environment we will face in the coming years. Both components provided essential information and began to prepare us for our roles in the strategic planning process that will get underway soon."

Some trustee seminars can be designed and staffed by in-house personnel. In other cases, the board should, together with management, invite outside experts from time to time to deepen the trustees' knowledge. For college and university boards, for instance, specialists might offer sessions on instructional technology, market demographics, employment forecasts, the competitive landscape, or public policy toward private education.

Study Groups

Study groups are subsets of trustees, sometimes supplemented by experts not on the board, charged expressly to become well versed on a particular topic and to then share that knowledge with the board as a whole. In one instance that concerned divestment, trustees on a college board visited advocates and opponents of divestiture, consulted with financial advisers, systematically reviewed the relevant literature, and then presented the "weight of evidence" to the board. Another university appointed a study group, with several specialists not on the board, to consider whether or not to outsource certain administrative operations. And a state university system's board of regents convened a public, half-day study session, facilitated by a national expert, on the future of academic tenure and the alternatives.

Obviously, study groups are aided by the presence of individuals with a professional knowledge of the issues. That talent need not, however, be external to the board. The more effective boards deliberately appoint a few trustees with relevant experiences and expertise; for example, some college boards include presidents or professors from comparable, noncompetitive colleges or executives from educational foundations or associations. Such appointments offer the board an internal source of knowledge and, despite the concerns of some educators, we encountered no situation where these individuals attempted to assume the role of a surrogate president or to exert undue influence.

Committee Rotation

Committee rotation is an attractive option to extend the sphere of trustees' expertise. (Reconfiguring or restructuring committees, as discussed in Chapter 5, also has a beneficial effect on trustee education.) Too often, board members develop depth of knowledge, without breadth, due to lengthy terms on a single committee. Almost every board has the legendary wizards of physical plant, investment, audit, or academic affairs. Far fewer boards have trustees with a broad span of knowledge.

In order to expand the trustees' scope of knowledge, several of the Trustee Demonstration Project boards elected to rotate trustee committee assignments. No one was compelled to rotate, and everyone was afforded an occasion to express preferred committee memberships. However, mindful of the purpose of the policy—to expand the trustees' knowledge base—board members were strongly encouraged to accept new assignments approximately every three or four years, with exceptions allowed for committee chairs and others to complete a long-term objective such as a capital campaign or a five-year plan.

Almost all trustees and senior staff viewed these changes positively. The most frequently mentioned benefit was the "opportunity to understand all aspects of the college," and "the broadening of trustees' vision and understanding of the institution." Others cited the value of not "settling down in one place," of "opening up positions for new blood," and of "infusing committees with new ideas." One president summarized well the advantages of rotation:

> It required people getting out of their little corners, the areas that they had learned and "owned." They used to say "I'll take care of the endowment." They wanted to work on what they knew best, and leave the rest to others. We had to rotate them around, they had to learn everything, in order to properly govern the institution as a whole board. . . . They've moved away

from being the guardians of the physical plant, overseers of the administration, and "deep pockets."

Rotation of committee assignments was a relatively modest change that yielded a rather substantial dividend in the form of trustee education.

The approaches to board education presented thus far are designed to enable boards to self-identify areas where, individually or collectively, they lack sufficient knowledge. However, were boards to do only that, a problem would remain. Organizational theorists sometimes refer to this difficulty as the D.K.D.K. syndrome, mistakes that arise because people "Don't Know what they Don't Know." Frequently, these are costly errors. In *Competing for the Future*, a book on corporate strategy, Hamel and Prahalad (1994) remark:

> The . . . greater hazard is that individuals don't know what they don't know and, worse yet, don't know that they don't know. This is the great challenge for every organization: How do we come to know what we don't know? How can we identify, and then transcend, the boundaries to our own knowledge? The well-worn aphorism—what you don't know *can* hurt you—is entirely apropos. (1994, 52)

Unaware of their own knowledge gaps, boards of trustees are prone to the same syndrome and the same risks.

To avert or at least minimize this predicament, trustees must be certain to extend beyond the boardroom and beyond the executive suite efforts to identify crucial knowledge gaps. To learn what the board does not know it does not know may entail conversations with key stakeholders.

Boards must not be reluctant to seek knowledge from sources other than the administration. To the contrary, trustees should be wary of a CEO who hesitates to foster such events. Just as no student can learn everything from a single professor, no board can be adequately enlightened by one executive. Fortunately, there are productive ways for trustees to learn that do not compromise the CEO's authority or status.

Literature and Conferences

Literature and conferences may be the simplest and most direct approach to trustee education. At a minimum, board members could be provided subscriptions to the basic trade journals. For college or university boards, these would include *The Chronicle of Higher Education*, a weekly newspaper, and *Trusteeship*, a bimonthly periodical of the Association of Governing Boards. Two other informative and accessible magazines for such boards are *Change*, issued bimonthly by the American Association for Higher Education, and *Educational Record*, a quarterly publication of the American Council on Education. The Association of Governing Boards (AGB) and the National Center for Nonprofit Boards (NCNB) also publish numerous brochures and pamphlets on governance and trusteeship, applicable to a broad range of nonprofit organizations.[1] In addition, an institution's staff might selectively clip articles from the popular press and excerpt or summarize articles from professional journals that would broaden or deepen the trustees' understanding of the institution or profession. On occasion, an article from any of these sources could form the basis for a focused dinner conversation or a trustee mini-seminar. Stated a college president, "We give trustees some of the booklets to read at home and then follow up with some discussion of the main points as they apply here on this campus."

Conferences provide another avenue for trustee education. AGB offers a national conference annually, as well as a host of specialized seminars on topics such as finance, planning, enrollment management, academic affairs, and development. (The National Association of Independent Schools has a similar array of programs for member institutions.) Some boards encourage trustees to attend these conferences together, which augments both the educational and social benefits. Many boards ask trustees to report briefly to the entire board the most important information and the best ideas presented at the meeting.

Peer Education

Peer education has long been recognized by educators as one of the most beneficial resources for students. Trustees, too, can learn a great deal from one another, especially from colleagues on the boards of similar organizations. "For me, the real value of conferences," noted one board member, "has been the interchange with other trustees, to hear how they approach and solve problems. In the formal sessions, most people hold back, but during informal get-togethers, especially if people stay overnight, they are more forthcoming on a one-to-one or small-group basis."

Conversations with members of other boards partially compensate for the relatively limited frame of reference of most trustees. Among college and university trustees, only a small minority have served on more than one college board. (Indeed, few trustees serve on more than one board of the same type of agency or institution.) The lack of a comparable perspective leads board members to erroneous conclusions, such as a sense that the problems their college faces are unique or, conversely, that the problems are unavoidable. Likewise, trustees have little awareness that there are better (or at least different) ways to do the board's business. Conversations with peers on other boards have proven to be a constructive and enjoyable means to overcome the trustees' isolation and lack of knowledge. In fact, among the project demonstration sites, the annual "summit" of the board chairs and college presidents (as described in Chapter 1) was rated by the participants as among the project's most effective interventions. To quote one of the participants:

> I was an auto dealer. Every Chevy dealer operates differently. The best thing that happened to me was talking to other dealers about how they handled things. Each was different, but each knew how to succeeed. In this demonstration project, the best was talking to other board chairs. . . . Talking with peers about enrollments, budgeting, information systems—I learned from that.

Happily, a college need not be included as part of an action research project to reap the benefits of peer education. There are numerous other alternatives.

- Several institutional consortia arrange for an annual meeting of board chairs and, sometimes, the chairs of key committees. Topics range from substance (e.g., deferred maintenance, student financial aid, and multiculturalism) to process (board committee structure, avenues of communication with stakeholders, and trustee evaluations).
- The Association of Governing Boards (AGB) and the National Association of Independent Schools (NAIS) each sponsors an annual conference for teams of board chairs and CEOs. Both programs provide opportunities for the chairs to meet separately to share successes and setbacks, and problems and solutions.
- Numerous networks of colleges or schools have cosponsored one-day workshops for trustees from local institutions. In a typical format, the trustees meet together for several hours to discuss common concerns about governance or education, and then convene as individual boards later in the day to consider the specific application of ideas exchanged in the earlier plenary session.

Despite the value that trustees attach to peer education, remarkably few institutions structure such occasions. As a result, many boards bypass an educational opportunity that promises multiple benefits for trustees at a low, shared cost to the participating institutions.

Firsthand Experiences

As a rule, trustees do not experience firsthand the life of an institution. In fact, board members are regularly counselled to remain suitably aloof from the daily occurrences on campus. Knowledge, therefore, normally comes through vicarious experiences when, for instance, an actual participant describes a particular event or activity. However, firsthand experience, or at least direct observation, can be an effective teacher, as one university president noted:

> No matter how much we talk about policy, trustees need to be in the messy business so that they understand the context. Trustees can't be global and strategic without going through some of the blood and gore that underlies the issue. But then they have to make the policy and walk away from the gore. It takes a lot of knowledge and a lot of discipline.

To illustrate the instructive value of direct experiences by trustees, we cite a few examples from higher education:

- In order to ensure that trustees better understood a newly adopted common curriculum for all first-year students, the president of one college asked that the faculty members responsible for this approach teach a module to board members in "classes" of a dozen or so. Materials on the topic, civil disobedience, were distributed in advance and a spirited discussion characterized each class section.
- At one project site, where the college had under review the possibility of a new library, the staff organized a one-day bus tour for trustees to visit three other campuses, where each had taken a very different approach to facilities and technology. (An added dividend of the excursion was, the trustees reported, that the board had the chance to socialize and cohere.)
- At two universities where the board was unclear about the nature, rigor, and scope of the tenure review process, the administration provided a "walk-through" of actual dossiers (edited to ensure anonymity). The goal was *not* to immerse trustees in tenure decisions but, quite to the contrary, to demonstrate to the board the depth and stringency of the quality-control process.
- At a liberal arts college, the president decided that the board would be unable to appreciate either the science curriculum or the institution's facility needs without a firsthand view. "We realized that we needed to take the trustees out to the science facility, to meet with faculty members, so that they really understand what is going on."

We have encountered dozens of other examples that ranged from participation in a portion of a freshman Outward Bound experience, to participation in a campus-wide day of public service, to a hands-on lesson with computer-aided instruction. Events such as these render vivid and concrete ideas that trustees may not entirely grasp as abstract concepts explained through second-hand reports.

Direct Communications with Key Constituents

Trustees have historically been overreliant on secondary sources of information. Boards and administrators alike traditionally regarded face-to-face communication with constituents as inappropriate for trustees. Such conversations might corrode the authority of senior officers, obscure the distinction between governance and management, open the floodgates of criticisms, and create forums where the shrillest voices, rather than the best minds, would prevail.

These were the lessons learned from the corporate sector, where most CEOs deplored and opposed two-way communication between individual directors, on the one hand, and shareholders, employees, and customers on the other hand. By and large, corporate directors (often CEOs themselves) were sympathetic to these arguments.

That argument no longer obtains (Chait 1995). To be entirely dependent upon a single source of information created risks that most directors no longer wished to assume. Boards realized that direct communication with stakeholders provided an important means to become smarter directors—to understand better the perspectives, concerns, and assessments of various constituents, and to understand better the corporation's culture, performance, and challenges. As John Aram, a professor of strategy at Case Western Reserve University and an expert on corporate governance, observes:

> Directors should know something about the company down at the grassroots level. Know the products and how they're made. Go out to the plant, meet the employees and the customers there, get to know the community and the stakeholders. So when they're thinking about strategic moves, they will have accumulated knowledge about what the corporation really is. (Aram 1996, 13)

As a practical matter, boards of directors sometimes had no real choice about two-way communication as institutional investors with large stakes in the company demanded an audience with the board. Now, various boards of directors, e.g., General Motors, Home Depot, and Digital Equipment Corporation, meet routinely with institutional investors, middle managers, and customers.

The project sites and other colleges where we served as consultants have followed a similar path as the trustees recognized the value of closer contact with constituents. In one case, the realization emerged from a self-assessment that revealed as a key concern "the board's limited connectedness to the college's communities." In another instance, the issue, as one trustee reported, surfaced at a retreat where the board "focused on how to draw closer to the faculty."

"How do you build commitment on a board?" one college trustee, an expert on corporate governance, asked rhetorically. "You have the board interface with instructors and students as frequently as possible. You have to see who you are working for, on whose behalf you are doing this. I want to hear comments about strengths and weaknesses firsthand."

What has enabled trustees to learn more from stakeholders and, therefore, to govern better?[2] The most useful actions cited by trustees were mechanisms and activities that created opportunities for board members and stakeholders to collaborate on significant, substantive tasks. "I believe that over all the years that I've been a trustee, the best way to build relationships with the faculty is through working together on something meaningful." This view was seconded by a trustee of a different college. "We tried dinners with trustees and faculty to improve community relations. These were good occasions, but not the best use of our time or the faculty's. We decided to work harder to have our time together be meaningful work rather than a social context. You build more respect by working together." The form that the work assumed varied; the constant was the seriousness of purpose.

Some boards—Cornell College, Denison University, Goucher, Franklin and Marshall, Wellesley, and Wittenberg, to name a few—established special, multiconstituency *task forces* to develop a strategic plan. Usually over the course of a year, these groups, together and as subcommittees (and with staff support), conducted environmental scans and internal self-assessments and identified strategic opportunities and initiatives. Some even drafted the plan.

On other campuses, the vehicle for collaborative learning was a presidential *search committee*. The very nature of this task dictated that trustees listen and learn about constituents' perspectives on the institution's mission, priorities, and leadership requirements. "Faculty, staff, students, and board members served, and when you work together as long and as hard as we did, you get to know each other pretty well. We had open and frank discussions and consensus was reached. It was a great process."

On many campuses, constituents serve as *members or representatives* on trustee committees, most notably, student and academic affairs committees, usually without a vote. Discussions with students and faculty provide occasions for trustees to be better and independently informed; constituents are particularly well-positioned to answer directly and credibly many questions board members have about the students' educational experiences or about the academic profession.[3] Discussions with faculty, for example, have enriched the board's knowledge about academic labor markets, dual-career families, shifts in sources and levels of funded research, and the process of curriculum development. On one board, the chair of the faculty senate, the president of the student assembly, and the head of the parents' association all attend and serve as representatives on every committee. As one trustee at this university noted, the benefits are mutual: "They serve in a reporting capacity, so we learn from them, but they are also witnessing the board in action, and can take back to their groups what they have learned from us."

Beyond the formal structure of the board, many institutions have created less formal methods to be informed by stakeholders. One board meets annually with regional corporate leaders to learn whether the college's graduates and programs serve well the needs of the business community. The boards of several independent colleges have sponsored open forums to hear student views on tuition and fees, divestment, presidential selection procedures, and the quality of social life. Others arrange for trustees to visit dormitories or to dine at faculty homes prior to board meetings. These are not simply social occasions. "The dinners are a lot of fun, but their real value is that we get to talk outside the formal meeting setting about what is going on at the college," declared one college board member. This is *not* vigilantism on the part of individual trustees, as one vice chair was careful to emphasize. "You need to be out there walking around if you're going to govern responsibly. Otherwise, you're a captive of whatever the administration says. Once you determine anecdotally what's going on, you circle back and plug in your concerns at the appropriate place."

Despite the value most board members attach to two-way communication with constituents, not all presidents share that view. James Fisher (1991, 66–67), former president of Towson State University, decried the "ever closer relationships between boards and faculty, students, and staff." Regrettably, notes Fisher, boards have "granted faculty and students access and rights that were formerly privileges to be granted, denied, or withdrawn by college presidents." These "countless instances of board/faculty/student formal associations" have the potential, he argued, to "neuter" the presidency. Another university president boasted at an invitational seminar that "my trustees have to *earn* the right to talk to faculty, and vice versa."

Other presidents and trustees worry that greater commerce between boards and constituents will invite students and faculty to carp about a myriad of trivial issues or to reopen questions that the administration had already processed and settled. Unpersuaded by this argument, a trustee replied:

> If the CEO is reluctant to permit close contact with constituents, if the CEO and the staff are afraid to have a director talk to a plant manager, then the CEO hasn't done the job very well. Why not have students talk to trustees? What's there to hide? These are our clients. I'm old enough and smart enough to know that some people complain. Trustees are as qualified as the president to interpret the views expressed. The closer I get to reality, the better I can sympathize with and help the CEO.

LEARNING WHAT TO WATCH

Corporate boards accept axiomatically that directors are responsible for monitoring the financial performance and overall health of the company. Such reviews are routine and integral components of corporate board meetings. Gordon Donaldson, a professor at the Harvard Business School, recently extended this concept to include a "formal strategic-review process . . . within the existing governance process so that the board can exercise proactively its responsibility for strategic oversight" (1995, 101). Thus, a "strategic audit" would be conducted every three years (so as not to be confused with an annual operating review) under the leadership of a strategic audit committee composed exclusively of independent directors.

> The committee should select the criteria for review of strategic performance, oversee the design of the database, and establish a review process. It should ensure the integrity and continuity of the ongoing data collection and reporting efforts, identify issues for discussion with the CEO, keep the full board abreast of the evidence, and schedule both regular and special meetings. (Donaldson 1995, 106)

While some CEOs may resent a strategic audit as an unreasonable intrusion or an undue burden, Donaldson contends that the external pressures for vigilant, strategic oversight by directors offer no more attractive alternative. Furthermore, "ensuring that independent board members and the CEO meet in private and focus on objective evidence about the strategy in place is the best guarantee that well-informed, orderly, and timely strategic change will spring from the established governance process" (ibid., 107).

Unlike corporate boards, most boards of trustees for nonprofits do not systematically monitor critical institutional performance indicators. Many, of course, do attend seasonally to revenues and expenses, to development data, and to audited financial statements, although only a minority provide informative competitive comparisons. Far fewer still conduct a strategic audit or otherwise chart the institution's progress toward the attainment of strategic priorities. Rather, the typical board seems to endorse plans without mileposts and "transformations" without checkpoints.

Why are boards of trustees usually so lax in the discharge of a responsibility that is so important? First, whereas corporate directors understand performance measures related to the rate of return on shareholder investment, these same individuals, as trustees of nonprofit institutions, are uncertain about what matters most and how to "keep score," especially beyond the financial realm. Second, trustees are often overwhelmed with data—too much information about operations and too little analysis of the policy and strategy implications distilled from the data. As one trustee so concisely captured the problem, "We get lots of information, we just have no idea what it means." Finally, the steady turnover of trustees on most boards weakens the group's collective memory, a condition exacerbated by the absence of a policy digest or "legislative history" that summarizes the trustees' strategic decisions, the attendant policy objectives, and the proposed measures of success.

These circumstances impel most boards to monitor familiar operational realms on a short-term and noncomparative basis. Hence, boards generally focus heavily on market share, development, and budget data to the relative neglect of gauges of progress toward the realization of strategic priorities. In concert with senior management, the board of trustees must determine the strategic areas, appropriate criteria, and relevant benchmarks to monitor. When strategic initiatives or major policies are proposed, management should concurrently suggest (and, if not, the board should request) the means and measures that will be used to assess advancement toward the stated objectives. How will a college, for example, chart progress toward a revitalized undergraduate curriculum, more selective doctoral programs, greater diversity, state-of-the-art technology, international breadth, or expanded entrepreneurship? Unless progress can be calculated, the board cannot learn whether institutional strategy has succeeded, stalled, or failed—an unacceptable circumstance by any standard.

DEVELOPING DASHBOARDS

In order to ensure that boards receive vital information in a timely matter, many of the project sites created a "dashboard," a relatively simple yet exceptionally valuable tool.[4] Automotive dashboards include various dials, gauges, instruments, and "idiot lights," all intended to provide the driver with *selective* information essential to operate the vehicle safely. The console cannot display all information or be cluttered with extraneous information (e.g., the condition of the floormats or the available capacity of the glove compartment). The driver must be able to determine *at a glance* whether there are abnormal conditions that jeopardize the occupants, the vehicle, or the journey.

Automotive dashboards are not substitutes for drivers or windshields, any more than institutional dashboards are substitutes for leaders or vision. Nonetheless, both kinds of dashboards are crucial for learning about the capacity to proceed, the pace of progress, and potential problems.

The creation of a dashboard normally starts with an extended discussion among trustees and senior staff, as part of a regular board meeting or a retreat, about critical success factors—the most essential *areas of performance*. These are the variables that most determine whether the institution will flourish or falter. In higher education, these "strategic drivers" typically cluster around resource acquisition and management, program quality, and enrollment management. Taylor, Meyerson, and Massy (1993, xi) prefer the categories of financial capital, physical capital, information capital, and human capital.

Once the critical success factors have been identified, the board and the executive officers can then propose and consider strategic performance indicators—the qualitative and quantitative data that most accurately measure and convey the *criteria of performance*. Although the indicators will vary from campus to campus, the "top 10," as determined by Taylor, Meyerson, and Massy (1993, xv), appear in Exhibit 4.1.

One project site selected some of these 10 and then added others including: racial/ethnic diversity, attrition and graduation rates, top 10 majors, average net revenue per student, and educational and general expenditures per student. In light of institutional strategy, another site incorporated among only eight performance indicators enrollment by gender and ratio of in-state to out-of-state students. A prestigious research-oriented university decided that the dashboard should display funded research per faculty FTE, number of faculty appointed members of national academies, and publications per faculty FTE. In short, dashboards need to be locally constructed to serve local needs.

**Top Ten Institutional Performance Indicators
for Colleges and Universities**

1. Overall Revenue Structure
2. Overall Expenditure Structure
3. Excess (Deficit) of Current Fund Revenues over Current Fund Expenditures
4. Percent of Freshman Applicants Accepted and Percent of Accepted Freshmen Who Matriculate
5. Ratio of Full-Time Equivalent Students to Full-Time Equivalent Faculty
6. Institutional Grant Aid as a Percent of Tuition and Fee Income
7. Tenure Status of Full-Time Equivalent Faculty
8. Percent of Full-Time Equivalent Employees Who Are Faculty
9. Maintenance Backlog as a Percent of Total Replacement Value of Plant
10. Percent of Living Alumni Who Have Given at Any Time during the Past Five Years

EXHIBIT 4.1

The third step in the process requires that the board and the staff set the benchmarks that define the desired standards of performance. The key decisions are to determine the relevant bases for comparisons and then to establish appropriate levels of performance. Should effectiveness be calibrated by industry norms, best practices, a generic (e.g., liberal arts colleges) or specific (e.g., the Associated Colleges of the Midwest) peer group, past performance (trend lines), or some combination thereof? Comparative/competitive data on higher education are remarkably readily available from the federal government's Integrated Postsecondary Education Data System (IPEDS), from the Association of Governing Boards (Taylor et al. 1991), and through various institutional consortia and data exchange compacts. With respect to levels of performance, the board and staff should assign minimal tolerances—ranges or thresholds that delimit the boundaries of acceptable performance. In addition, of course, the institution may establish some "stretch" targets or an aspirational level of performance. As a result of the discussions about the areas, criteria,

Select Gauges from the Dashboard of "Midwest University"

MIDWEST UNIVERSITY
Report Structure

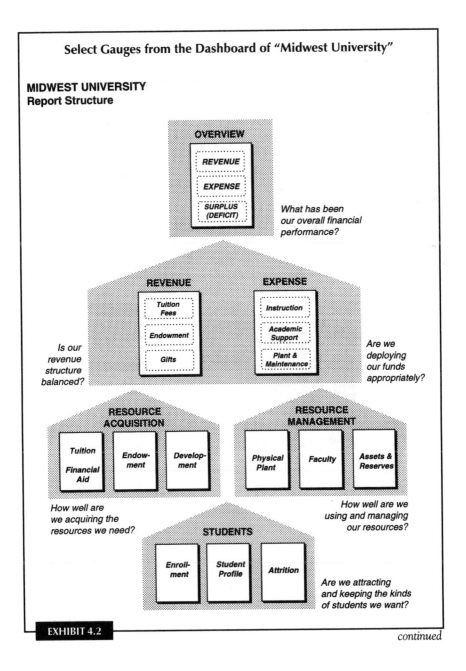

EXHIBIT 4.2

continued

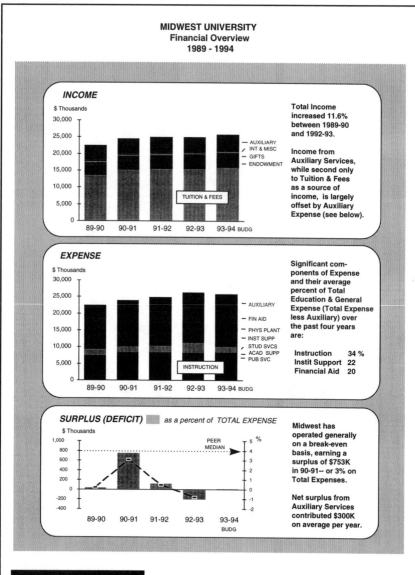

MIDWEST UNIVERSITY
Financial Overview
1989 - 1994

INCOME

$ Thousands

Total Income increased 11.6% between 1989-90 and 1992-93.

Income from Auxiliary Services, while second only to Tuition & Fees as a source of income, is largely offset by Auxiliary Expense (see below).

EXPENSE

$ Thousands

Significant components of Expense and their average percent of Total Education & General Expense (Total Expense less Auxiliary) over the past four years are:

Instruction   34 %
Instit Support   22
Financial Aid   20

SURPLUS (DEFICIT) as a percent of TOTAL EXPENSE

$ Thousands

Midwest has operated generally on a break-even basis, earning a surplus of $753K in 90-91-- or 3% on Total Expenses.

Net surplus from Auxiliary Services contributed $300K on average per year.

EXHIBIT 4.2 (continued)

continued

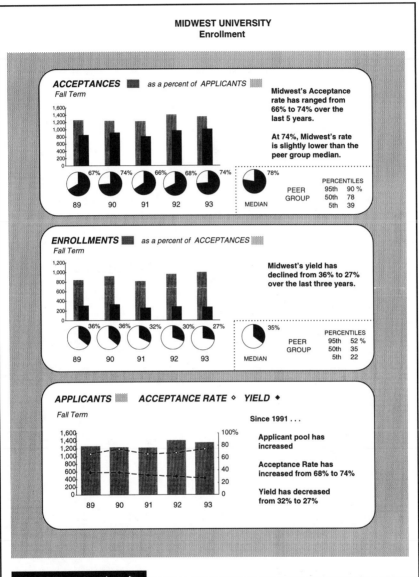

MIDWEST UNIVERSITY
Enrollment

ACCEPTANCES ▓ *as a percent of APPLICANTS* ▓
Fall Term

Midwest's Acceptance rate has ranged from 66% to 74% over the last 5 years.

At 74%, Midwest's rate is slightly lower than the peer group median.

	PERCENTILES	
PEER GROUP	95th	90 %
	50th	78
	5th	39

ENROLLMENTS ▓ *as a percent of ACCEPTANCES* ▓
Fall Term

Midwest's yield has declined from 36% to 27% over the last three years.

	PERCENTILES	
PEER GROUP	95th	52 %
	50th	35
	5th	22

APPLICANTS ▓ **ACCEPTANCE RATE** ◇ **YIELD** ◆
Fall Term

Since 1991 . . .

Applicant pool has increased

Acceptance Rate has increased from 68% to 74%

Yield has decreased from 32% to 27%

EXHIBIT 4.2 (continued)

continued

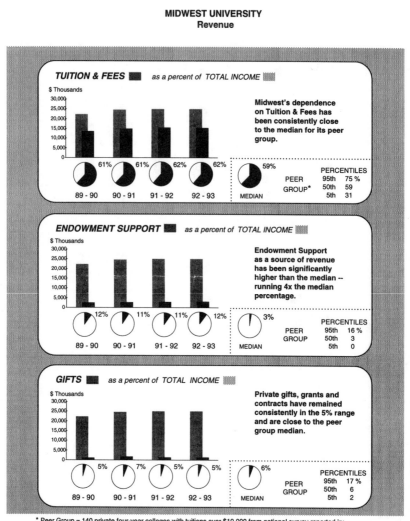

MIDWEST UNIVERSITY
Revenue

TUITION & FEES ■   *as a percent of TOTAL INCOME* ▦

$ Thousands

Midwest's dependence
on Tuition & Fees has
been consistently close
to the median for its peer
group.

				PERCENTILES	
	61% 61% 62% 62%		59% PEER GROUP*	95th	75 %
89 - 90	90 - 91 91 - 92 92 - 93	MEDIAN	50th	59
			5th	31

ENDOWMENT SUPPORT ■   *as a percent of TOTAL INCOME* ▦

$ Thousands

Endowment Support
as a source of revenue
has been significantly
higher than the median --
running 4x the median
percentage.

				PERCENTILES	
	12% 11% 11% 12%		3% PEER GROUP	95th	16 %
89 - 90	90 - 91 91 - 92 92 - 93	MEDIAN	50th	3
			5th	0

GIFTS ■   *as a percent of TOTAL INCOME* ▦

$ Thousands

Private gifts, grants and
contracts have remained
consistently in the 5% range
and are close to the peer
group median.

				PERCENTILES	
	5% 7% 5% 5%		6% PEER GROUP	95th	17 %
89 - 90	90 - 91 91 - 92 92 - 93	MEDIAN	50th	6
			5th	2

* Peer Group = 140 private four-year colleges with tuitions over $10,000 from national survey reported in:
Taylor, Meyerson and Massey, *Strategic Indicators for Higher Education: Improving Performance.*
Princeton, NJ: Peterson's Guides, 1993.

EXHIBIT 4.2 (continued)

and standards of performance, the staff then develops a prototype dashboard. The console will undoubtedly undergo periodic modifications and revisions as the board's experiences dictate and as the institution's circumstances change. Over time, the sophistication of the design and the utility of the information will escalate. Witness, for instance, Exhibit 4.2, which displays an overview and 9 of the 20 panels that constitute the dashboard of Midwest University, a pseudonym for an institution that participated in the Board Information System (Butler, Hirsch, and Swift 1995).

No matter how refined, dashboards are, in fact, passive devices. Unless trustees regularly review the information displayed and consider the implications, the dashboard will not influence the board's focus, actions, and decisions. There are two modes of review: routine and nonroutine. In the routine mode, the board establishes a regular calendar of events linked to the dashboard. Usually on an annual cycle, major trustee committees present, analyze, and discuss with the entire board a particular cluster of dashboard indicators and perhaps some secondary yardsticks. This approach establishes a rhythm of reports and ensures periodic attention by the whole board to critical success factors.

The nonroutine mode can be characterized as governance by exception or by "trip wire." If and when an indicator exceeds the established parameters of acceptable performance, that event would automatically activate an inquiry and possible action by the board or the appropriate committee to remedy the problem.

Of all the tools and techniques that we have introduced to boards of trustees across the not-for-profit sector, none has been more universally or more enthusiastically received than dashboards. The benefits of dashboards are multiple and considerable.

Metaphorically, visually, and substantively, dashboards are an unsurpassed means for trustees to learn what to watch. Even more importantly, the very construction and continuous refinement of the dashboard requires, as no other exercise quite does, that the board and staff collectively and collaboratively discover what matters most. And because the dashboard alerts trustees to the vital signs of institutional health, it "helps the trustees stay focused on significant issues," as one president remarked. Moreover, dashboards eliminate, or at least abbreviate, many unnecessary conversations because, as long as the gauges indicate that conditions are well within acceptable ranges, there may be no reasons to discuss, for example, admissions, budgets, or tenure practices. Time can be allocated instead to other strategic concerns that do require attention or to emergent, future-oriented issues.

CONCLUSION

To summarize, effective boards consciously create abundant opportunities for their trustees to learn about the institution, the relevant profession(s), and the larger environment. Some events aim to enlighten the entire board, while others are designed to serve a particular committee or newer trustees. Trustee education occurs on and off campus, with and without outside experts. The most successful programs are characterized by

- multiple opportunities and varied formats methodically and mutually orchestrated by the board and the administration
- content clearly germane to the institution's priorities and the trustees' portfolio
- direct access to the perspectives of crucial constituencies, especially through collaboration on meaningful tasks

Trustees would do well to heed John Aram's admonition to corporate board members:

> Directors need to recognize what preparation means—not just reviewing the budget statements and the financials but understanding the inner workings of the company. They should also recognize whether or not they're fully informed. . . . [I]f board members are not informed, they're not being responsible. (Aram 1996, 13)

NOTES

1. AGB: Suite 400, One Dupont Circle, Washington, D.C., 20036; (202) 296-8400. NCNB: Suite 510, 2000 L St., NW, Washington, D.C., 20036; (202) 452-6262.

2. In Chapter 5 of *The Effective Board of Trustees* (Chait, Holland, and Taylor 1991), we explain the value of constructive board-constituent relations to the overall political climate and to organizational morale. We are concerned here, however, with the value of these relationships to the board's efforts to be well informed.

3. We do not recommend that students currently enrolled or faculty currently employed at an institution serve as a member of that college's board because of the potential conflict of interest. On the other hand, recent graduates and faculty currently employed at a comparable, noncompetitive institution would be valuable additions to the board. An AGB 1991 survey indicated that 24% of public college boards and 10% of private college boards include student members; for faculty the percentages respectively are 7% and 14%. Many boards and presidents appreciate the presence of another incumbent or former college president as a trustee. These individuals add experience and insight and often serve as a useful check against drift by the board into trivial matters.

4. The exact origins of the "dashboard" concept are obscure. We first learned of the idea from Richard Umbdenstock, President and CEO, Providence Services, Spokane, Washington. Lawrence Butler, Chairman of The Cheswick Center in Rockville, Maryland, has significantly advanced the state of the art through the development of a Board Information System.

CHAPTER 5

Doing Business Better As a Board

M ost boards are legally organized to act only as a corporate body assembled at a duly constituted meeting. Yet, despite the centrality of meetings as *the* venue to govern, most trustees complain that board meetings are boring and inconsequential, especially given the strategic issues and turbulent environment that may confront the institution. When we ask trustees and CEOs to reflect honestly on how their institution would be affected if the board disappeared altogether, a disquieting number respond that the actions of a few individual trustees would be missed, but that the institution would barely notice if the board, as a board, simply stopped meeting, as long as there was a competent CEO at the helm.

While trustees are legally obligated to discharge certain business, such as hiring a president and adopting a budget, a board can, as some do, meet infrequently and adjourn quickly. Several college boards meet as seldom as twice a year for two or three hours. And why not? This calendar may be preferable to three or four two-day meetings that do nothing to enhance the institution's strategic position. Better to waste a little time than a lot.

On the other hand, better boards not only meet more often, typically three or four two-day meetings annually, but meet more purposefully to pursue critical issues and to extract the greatest benefits from the trustees' talent. These boards reject the claim that "meetings are meetings" with intrinsic and intractable problems. In the spirit of continuous quality improvement that so many boards commend to faculty and staff, these boards strive to do business better.

If a board wants to "do business" better, trustees must identify and stay focused on strategic priorities, use board and committee meetings intention-ally to pursue those issues, structure the board to pursue consequential work, and acquire information that will inform strategic decision making. These are the tasks that define the work of a value-adding board.

FOCUSING THE BOARD'S ATTENTION

Boards and trustee committees frequently squander scarce time on issues with little or no long-term significance, while matters of real consequence are ignored. A few examples, all from well-regarded institutions, are sufficient to illustrate the problem:

- A university finance committee adopted a quarter-billion-dollar budget with virtually no debate, except for an hour-long discussion about why the return on campus vending machines was not higher.
- A trustee committee used most of a meeting to discuss whether or not to install an answering machine in an administrative office.
- A board heard a report from the buildings and grounds committee about the placement of landscaping and then debated for over an hour the hardiness of certain shrubs when planted in that part of the country.
- A discussion at a board meeting extended not only to where to hold the annual trustee banquet but to the selection of a subgroup to sample the menu at the proposed site.
- A protracted discussion at a physical plant committee meeting revolved around what type of file cabinets to place in staff offices, and whether to trim or uproot a tree adjacent to the site for a proposed new building.

Even more common than vapid discussions about trivial matters are long periods during which trustees passively listen to reports that could have been distributed and read prior to the meeting, assuming the information was worthy of the board's attention in the first place. One president did regularly mail a written update on campus issues to trustees in advance, *but* then read the report aloud anyway at the board meeting. Actions like this prompted a trustee to wonder, "When I get back on the plane after a meeting, I think, Why did I come? I didn't make any real contribution."

Practically any board member can relate comparable experiences, and even those engrossed in heated debates about mundane issues later ask, "Why did we do that? How did we get off on that tangent?" Probably because the board and the staff had not taken specific, deliberate actions to focus the trustees' attention on matters of consequence.

Starting with Strategy

The process starts with an overall sense of institutional strategy, shared by trustees and the CEO. "What's the big picture? That is what a board should be talking about," declared a long-time trustee. How does a board develop an overall sense of strategy? The trustees first ask the CEO to paint "the big picture"; to describe succinctly, orally and in a written outline, the institution's major opportunities and challenges and, against that backdrop, the most appropriate goals and strategies. This working document and presentation, developed in concert with senior staff, should serve as the basis for an in-depth discussion between the board and the CEO: Is the report clear and comprehensive? Is the CEO's take on the environment correct? Is something missing? Is this the kind of institution we want to be? Are these the most promising strategies? What can the board do *as a board* to help realize this vision for the institution?

An explicit discussion of institutional strategy should be a mandated event, whether at a retreat or a regular meeting devoted entirely, or nearly so, to this one topic. From this discussion should emerge a *continuous agenda*, a select list of "strategic drivers" or issues of paramount importance to the institution's success. These are matters, such as market position, financial equilibrium, multiculturalism, and technology, that will neither suddenly disappear nor be immediately resolved. Instead, they occupy the "bull's eye" on the board's target of attention.

At one college board's annual retreat, a relatively new president reviewed the institution's market niche, academic programs, and the possible dimensions and priorities of a capital campaign. For each topic, the president suggested specific roles that the board might play. After general reactions and questions from the board, the trustees convened in small discussion groups to reflect further on the issues the president raised, to consider alternative courses of action, and to assess the implications of the president's presentation for the board's continuous agenda.

This president's predecessor had long kept the board at arm's length and filled its agendas with trivia. A veteran trustee welcomed "the breath of fresh air" the new president provided, and then allowed, "I'm not proud to admit this, but until this year, the board had no idea what was really going on here. [The new president's] first presentation to the board just blew us away. We realized for the first time that we're facing some real problems, but our confidence is growing that the board can work with the president to solve these problems. Learning where the problems are was the first step."

Boards that are reasonably well informed about the institution and the environment can help develop the list of topics that should constitute the continuous agenda, rather than depend entirely on the institution's president and senior staff. At a retreat, for example, one board created and rank ordered a list of institutional challenges through a series of successive votes in which the issues considered less important were eliminated. The trustees eventually identified the handful of issues—the continuous agenda—that the majority agreed would be most likely to affect the institution's future.

Institutionalizing a Strategic Focus

A single discussion, a clever exercise, or a one-shot retreat will not keep a board steadily attuned to strategy. Indeed, board performance often falters because trustees are unable to integrate the conclusions of general discussions about strategy and institutional goals into the board's regular work and normal routines.

To do that requires a second type of agenda, a *derivative agenda*. As the name implies, the content derives directly from the continuous agenda and provides a crosswalk from strategic priorities to board activities. The derivative agendas typically take the form of annual work plans for each board committee (distributed to all board members) and charges to special task forces. These mechanisms help ensure that the lion's share of the board's time and energy will be devoted to matters clearly related to "the big picture."

Several years ago, one college's board made a commitment to hold an annual retreat to review the college's strategy and performance. The 1995 retreat centered around marketing, pricing, and student recruitment—all vital elements for a tuition-dependent college. At the retreat, both small groups and plenary sessions addressed the implications of changes in the external environment, potential responses to any decline in tuition income, and actions to solidify the college's market position and recruitment strategies. Most important, after the board had aired all the issues, the trustees translated the discussion into a series of specific assignments for the board and for standing committees and task forces (Exhibit 5.1). This final step, which too many boards omit, establishes the crucial linkage between the priorities of the institution and the work of the board.

A senior administrator at a university that adopted this approach a few years ago commented, "The net effect . . . has been a move from the board being involved in every aspect of the institution, no matter how unimportant, to trustees being quite intentional about where to focus their efforts."

A College's Board and Committee Goals for 1994–95

Primary Board Goals (Commitments for the Board as a Whole)

1. To continue the public phase of the capital campaign, with extensive trustee involvement in cultivation and solicitation activities and with total gifts and pledges to the campaign to reach $25 million by June 30.
2. To address the growing gap between the cost of the college's tuition and what the typical family can afford to pay (a) by completing the study of the Trustee Task Force on Marketing, Pricing, and Financial Aid by the October board meeting, with specific recommendations that can be implemented by the administration; (b) by mobilizing support for maximum impact on the state

EXHIBIT 5.1

continued

legislature in response to the coordinated statewide lobbying plan already developed by the Institutional Advancement Committee; (c) by studying the college's staffing plan to determine if there are alternative approaches that might enable the college to deliver its educational program at a lower unit cost; (d) by exploring alternative sources of funding for the college through entrepreneurial activities that build on our strengths and that do not carry an unacceptable level of risk; and (e) by exploring the possibility of additional student loan programs for our students that are funded from private sector sources.

Secondary Board Goals (Assigned to Board Committees or Task Forces)

1. To complete the process for planning the new library and technological infrastructure to the point that an architect for the project can be engaged by the end of the calendar year and given the program specifications necessary to design the building (to task force).
2. To upgrade the appearance of the campus with particular attention to (a) completing the loop road; (b) landscaping key areas of high visibility on campus; and (c) making visible improvements in the appearance of areas around the dormitories and in those areas normally included in the walking tour taken by prospective students and parents (to Buildings and Grounds Committee).
3. To achieve our faculty salary goals set in the long-range plan by 1995 (to Finance and Academic Affairs Committees).
4. To initiate an evaluation of the college's academic and support programs, with particular attention to (a) using new and more relevant measures; and (b) recognizing changes in the external environment, including: an increasingly diverse student population, racially and ethnically; the international geopolitical economy; and technological developments that may augment the teaching and learning process (to the president and director of planning and institutional research, reporting then to the Academic Affairs Committee).
5. To review the college's career counseling and placement program and to devise and implement a plan for trustee assistance in seeking additional employment opportunities for graduates in area corporations (to subcommittee of Religious and Student Life Committee.)

Goals for Ongoing Board Operations

1. To increase the level of trustee participation in activities of the board of trustees as evidenced by (a) an average of at least 70 percent of the board in attendance at each board meeting; (b) each trustee fulfilling at least one special assignment as agreed to with the chair or president; and (c) 100 percent participation in the annual fund.
2. To become actively involved as trustees in telling the college's story to its broader constituency.

EXHIBIT 5.1 (continued)

Making Meetings Consequential

There can be no substitute for substance at board meetings, a truth that only reinforces the need to determine first what matters most. However, a relationship does exist between content and format—the two are not mutually exclusive. How, then, can the architecture of board meetings support the substance? What can be done to alleviate trustees' number one complaint: board meetings are boring, unproductive, and inconsequential. "I could be watching a haircut and have more fun," one trustee quipped.

Most of the scores of college and university board meetings that we have observed exhibited a basic uniformity, despite vastly different institutional characteristics and trustee demographics. The standard-issue board meeting opens with a series of committee meetings, of equal duration, dominated by staff reports about operational issues. A dinner with faculty, students, or staff follows. The next morning, the formal board meeting proceeds with roll call, acceptance of minutes, the president's report (often distributed in advance and then recapitulated), committee reports (in alphabetical order), old business, new business, and adjournment. Even when a board's schedule differs from this template, little variation occurs from one meeting to the next. Most boards follow a single pattern time after time, regardless of the circumstances. Small wonder that trustees leave most board meetings without a sense of accomplishment. As one said, "The fall meeting was typical. All but one hour was spent on routine things we have to do every year. For example, we have to approve the budget. But when you do eight or nine of these things, there is little time left for discussion or anything else."

Most trustees find retreats to be far more engaging and productive than regular board meetings. When asked why, trustees explain that retreats

- allow sustained attention to important strategic issues
- afford maximum opportunity for participation
- transcend the regular committee structure
- mix trustees and staff in diverse configurations
- liberate the board from routine and habit

Embedded in these observations about retreats are the keys to make board meetings more engrossing and more consequential.

Letting Form Follow Function

What is true of good architecture is also true of good board meetings: *Form follows function.* A "one size fits all" approach makes no sense for buildings or meetings. As the board's leaders and the institution's president plan each meeting, the first questions to ask are, "What are we trying to accomplish at this meeting?" and "How can we use the available time to achieve our purposes?" Instead, most are apt to ask, "How should we fill the time available *given* the structure of the meeting?"

The board of Bangor Theological Seminary developed a flexible meeting structure to empower trustees and to remain focused on significant issues. In an interview (Exhibit 5.2), former president Malcolm Warford described several innovations such as the placement of committee meetings *after* the board meeting and the use of different types of meetings for different purposes.

**Interview with Malcolm Warford, Former President,
Bangor Theological Seminary**

What were you trying to accomplish when you changed the way your board meetings were structured?
What we did was to reconceive what a board meeting is. It was a basic shift from defining it as a business meeting at which reports are heard and acted on to an event with several parts, each intended to accomplish a specific purpose.

What did the new structure look like?
The board started with a plenary session, a traditional meeting for business and action on the issues the board had been preparing and working on.

The second session was a seminar lasting from 90 minutes to two hours, focusing on a policy issue or an issue concerned with theology or education. For example, we had someone in to talk about governing board effectiveness. On another occasion, we had a theologian lead a conversation about the meaning of vocation in modern Christian life. We brought in a sociologist of religion to talk about changes occurring in Mainline Protestantism. The board received readings beforehand, and they prepared faithfully. We learned that trustees want to get their hands on the real stuff. They want to grapple with important issues and engage in ideas that matter, but you have to do it in a systematic and sustained way. The issues have to be central and the information usable—not just academic, off-to-the-side presentations.

The third portion of the meeting was a social event with students and faculty, an effort to build the larger community.

The fourth part—committee meetings—took place the next morning. Committees met for two or three hours. Before, when committees met prior to the board meeting, we found that decisions were made too quickly and without adequate preparation. Meeting *after* the full board was a way to slow deliberations down. It pushed committees to consider issues that lay ahead. They knew they didn't have to head right from their meeting into the board meeting with their recommendations in hand. Committee members learned that they were responsible for preparing the whole board to make intelligent decisions about important matters.

The fifth part of the meeting was what we called a "collegium," which others refer to as an executive session. The board met with the president, with no other staff present. Then, from time to time, the board would meet by itself, calling the president back into the room at the end. This gave me a chance to clear up any questions and to help close out the meeting and lay the groundwork for the next.

EXHIBIT 5.2

continued

> **We understand that each of your board meetings had a particular focus. How did that work?**
> Every summer the staff and board worked together to map out the framework for the forthcoming year. We outlined a theme for each board meeting, based on the strategic issues facing the seminary. There were always some surprises along the way, but we were able to follow through on our agenda. Examples of our themes included strategic planning, space needs, and the future of faculty tenure at the seminary.
>
> **With the benefit of hindsight, would you do anything differently?**
> Not really, but I would suggest being flexible about moving the pieces around. The order worked for us, but a board shouldn't be so rigid that it can't shift as circumstances warrant. Basically, the flow of the meeting was intentional. At each stage, we were trying to prepare the way for the plenary session at the next board meeting to be as creative and disciplined as possible. We were always anticipating and working ahead.
>
> **EXHIBIT 5.2 (continued)**

We have seen many boards revise the normal architecture of meetings in order to accomplish particular purposes. Several boards instituted *thematic meetings* devoted to a single issue. In one version, each trustee committee first considers the matter separately, and then the board meets as a whole to exchange perspectives. In another version, the trustees first meet in deliberately diverse small groups rather than as committees.

On one campus, where the university experienced substantial enrollment growth over the past several years, the theme was how to manage the growth. The academic affairs committee considered the impact of enrollment increases on class size and the quality of instruction; the finance committee examined revenue and expenditure trends, with special emphasis on the institution's growing financial aid burden; and the buildings and grounds committee studied the impact of additional students on the physical plant, most notably, the strains on residence halls and dining facilities.

At the board meeting, each committee reported, and the board as a whole then discussed the implications and possible courses of action such as an enrollment cap, a capital campaign to raise money for new facilities, and a trade-off between substantial raises for the faculty and a moratorium on any net additions to the size of the faculty. The board deliberately made no decisions about these issues. Rather, the discussions were translated into future agenda items and assignments for board committees.

Enamored by the idea of thematic meetings, the board of a preeminent research university formulated several possible sessions at a recent retreat:

- a joint meeting with the board of a neighboring public research university to discuss interinstitutional cooperation

- a joint meeting with the board of a high-tech firm to discuss the future of educational technology
- a meeting with civic leaders to discuss a joint effort to reverse the decay of the area adjacent to the campus
- a meeting in Latin America to symbolically proclaim the university's intention to concentrate on this region for international programs and activities

Other boards have built thematic meetings around multiculturalism, the future of medical education, the implications of technology, student demographics, a physical plant master plan, and the revitalization of undergraduate education. Thematic meetings reinforce the notion that only a relatively small number of truly determinative strategic issues merit in-depth consideration by the board. Moreover, because the theme drives committee discussions, the meeting becomes more than just the sum of the often unrelated and functional items that committees usually address. As the board sees the connections and ramifications among the academic, financial, student, and physical facets of an issue, the trustees are more likely to consider the issue from a strategic, rather than operational, perspective.

One board has a *lunch session* with faculty members at each meeting. These are not, like so many similar arrangements, intended for "show and tell" or as a "puff piece" about a particular department. Instead, there are hard-nosed conversations about the capabilities of the student body, developments in the academic discipline, the balance between research and teaching, capital and equipment needs, and the roles of faculty in areas such as community service and student advisement. The board chair explained, "Social occasions with faculty can be nice, but we've found that they aren't as useful as talking about the real business of the college—what we're all here for."

Members of this board are so interested in the faculty and the academic program that the trustees *tour and meet in academic facilities* as often as possible. For example, board members have met in the library, had box lunches in the chemistry wing of the new science building, and visited the dance studio and the language lab. These sites were consciously selected to highlight specific areas of strategic concern to the college. The meeting in the library focused on the many implications of a proposed computerized catalog. The visit to the language lab further educated trustees about the college's intensive efforts to prepare students for study abroad—a key element of the strategic plan.

Discussion Sessions

Typically, the only opportunities trustees have for substantive interchange are board and committee meetings. And because board meetings are so focused on reports and seemingly urgent business, little time generally remains for reflection or dialog. Devices to bring more trustees into discussions of important issues include open forums, plenary sessions, small-group discussions, and joint committee meetings.

One university board has made *open forums* a central feature of each meeting. These 60- to 90-minute plenary sessions, open to senior staff, are intended to discuss but not decide an important strategic issue. Topics discussed at recent open forums included student retention and the relationship between institutional quality and tuition pricing. With the advent of forums, said one trustee, "We now realize that our job is more than just committee work, so we shouldn't just be sitting there for the rest of the meeting and listening. The open forums emphasize that all trustees are part of the board as a whole and that everyone should have input into our decisions."

Plenary Sessions

These offer a means to engage the entire board on a key topic such as fundraising, marketing strategies, or student financial aid. Discussions can simultaneously educate the entire board and provide guidance to particular committees. At one university, for example, the finance committee presented each year a tuition recommendation to the board that, for all practical purposes, afforded no opportunity for the rest of the board to consider the larger issues that affected tuition levels. Because the "recommendation" of the finance committee was a *fait accompli*, other trustees felt excluded and peripheral. To combat that problem, the board decided last year to hold a plenary session to discuss the causes and effects of tuition increases and to develop "first principles" that would govern the finance committee's recommendation in the next year. These principles ranged from the philosophical (e.g., maintain diversity) to the pragmatic (e.g., hold institutionally funded financial aid below 25% of gross tuition income).

On another campus, trustees divided into *discussion groups* to continue a conversation, started in a plenary session, about enrollment management. After about an hour, the trustees reassembled to exchange ideas, concerns, and suggestions that emerged from the breakout groups. The president recalled, "Trustees really appreciated the sessions and learned from them. They also had the effect of making senior staff more attentive in our planning endeavors, because we knew we would have to be ready with a major presentation about whatever was on the agenda."

Trustees of a prominent liberal arts college meet regularly with faculty in discussion groups to consider topics such as financial aid policy and student outcomes assessment.

> At the beginning, a lot of us wondered how useful these discussions would be, but they turned out to be a wonderful way for all of us to talk in an intimate forum. Trustees were very impressed with the practicality of the faculty, and some faculty told me later that we trustees knew a lot more than they realized. We've come out of this process with much more

respect for one another and with some actual ideas for dealing with some sticky problems.

Thus, the form (small groups) served the functions (to better educate the board and to strengthen ties to a key constituency).

Joint Committee Meetings

These provide a means to consider issues that transcend the purview of a single committee. Recently, the finance and facilities committees of a board together reviewed the campus master plan, toured selected buildings, and discussed financial requirements and priorities in the physical plant area. Other boards have held joint meetings of the finance and academic affairs committees to discuss student financial aid policy, or of the student life and advancement committees to consider plans for enrollment marketing.

All of these devices, singly or in combination, can enlighten and empower trustees, build consensus, and make meetings more interesting and engaging. Plenary sessions and open forums reinforce the board's identity as a group with long-term and collective responsibility for an institution that cannot be effectively discharged by the quasi-independent, loosely coordinated actions of various committees. Joint committee meetings remind trustees that truly strategic issues, almost by definition, cross committee lines. Taken together, these alternative structures provide multiple forums to comprehend and consider important issues together—before a decision has been reached, for all intents and purposes, by one or another committee.

While these innovations have great merit, boards do not need to employ a different format each time the trustees meet. A more prudent approach would be to allow the institution's overall strategy and the purposes of a particular meeting to dictate the design, not vice versa. A board chair explained, "There's not really any pattern. Sometimes we use a normal committee format. Sometimes we present data and have a discussion. We use small groups if we are trying to brainstorm and generate ideas. But if we're trying to move toward closure on a major issue, we'll stay together."

Executive Sessions

An increasing number of boards schedule executive sessions, with or without the institution's CEO, as part of every board meeting. At one college, trustees consider two questions at the session: Are we doing all we can to support the president and advance the college's goals? and Are there any concerns anyone has that we should address before the matter becomes acute? Another college's board has executive sessions before and after the board meeting, a chance "to prebrief and debrief." The "before" session allows trustees to broach any especially delicate concerns or problems—without staff, students, or the press present—about issues scheduled for consideration. A board chair explained, "It's a small technique but it is enormously useful. If there are sensitive issues, they'll come up. It gives us a chance to sort of counsel each other. At the post-meeting sessions, we sometimes excuse the president." The board meets without the president to discuss the board's performance and to symbolically remind trustees that the board, and not the president, is ultimately responsible for the institution.

While the presidents of some institutions are uneasy about executive sessions that exclude the CEO, we would reiterate the need to provide a means for trustees to address concerns to the entire board that otherwise would be raised elsewhere (see also Chapter 2). When the board meets as a whole in executive session, the probability decreases that splinter groups will conduct "rump" executive sessions in the parking lot, in taxis to the airport, or over golf or bridge. Finally, presidents should derive some comfort from the fact that executive sessions frequently produce expressions of support, empathy, and appreciation for the CEO.

Managing Time

It takes time to understand and deliberate significant issues and, for most trustees, time may be the scarcest commodity of all. Therefore, boards must use the time available to the utmost effect. In the majority of cases, this means that the board must substitute high yield activities for low yield activities—meet smarter, not longer.[1] While time is not infinitely elastic, some boards have adopted techniques that allow for the more efficient use of the hours available. All of these devices signal to trustees that some issues are more important than others and therefore deserve extended consideration.

Although a simple notion, remarkably few boards place agenda items in priority order, so that the most important topics are addressed first (and well before some trustees grow restless or even depart). If pressed for time, the board can omit, postpone, or treat summarily the less important items at the end of the docket. As the experience of Bangor Theological Seminary suggests, the order of the agenda cues trustees that, for example, a plenary session on the nature of theological education holds more importance than a committee meeting.

Other boards assign explicit *time guidelines* for each report or discussion. While the board's leadership may occasionally misjudge the amount of time required for a particular discussion, the guidelines provide trustees with another cue about the relative significance of agenda items. Armed with that information, board members are more likely to conserve time for the most important issues and less likely to extend discussions of comparatively minor matters.

A number of boards now use a *consent agenda*, a splendid parliamentary device that packages together all routine, non-exceptional items that require board approval, though not necessarily board discussion. One board's policy stipulates, "Any item may be removed from the consent agenda for discussion by any voting member of the board of trustees." Typical consent agenda items for a college board include: approval of bylaw amendments for college organizations, acceptance of gifts, approval of various leaves of absence, authorization to enter into contracts and leases below a specified dollar limit, approval of new academic minors or revised majors, the establishment of "sister" college arrangements, the election of members and officers of board committees, the schedule of future meeting dates, and approval of funds for the purchase of certain capital equipment below a specified dollar level. Support materials for each consent agenda item are provided in advance to trustees, as necessary. Typically, the CEO and the board chair, and on some boards the executive committee, have the authority to designate items for the consent agenda.

The value of a consent agenda as a time saver cannot be overestimated. On every board, certain matters, however routine, invariably prompt inquiries and ideas from a few well-intentioned trustees. "How about the property at 5th and Maple as a temporary office for the capital campaign?" "Did we seek a bid on the president's new car from that dealer on the east side? I got a terrific deal there last year." A consent agenda insulates routine items from unnecessary discussion and militates against the inefficient use of time.

The Role of Leadership

To keep a board meeting focused and productive requires skillful leadership, especially by the CEO and the board chair, and to a lesser extent by committee chairs and senior staff liaisons to board committees. The board's leaders and the institution's staff must plan thoughtfully and follow up diligently. Below, we address separately the roles of the CEO and the chair, but the pair must learn to "dance" together. If board meetings are orchestrated (i.e., coordinated rather than scripted), then the chair might be viewed as the conductor and the CEO or president as the featured soloist. Neither can stray far from the other's gaze or proceed independently.

The Institution's President

The president is the key player prior to board meetings. He or she works with the chair to identify the issues, to ensure adherence to the board's annual work plan, and to structure the time available. In addition, the president largely determines the information to be provided to trustees and coordinates staff support for board committees.

At the meeting, the president should engage the trustees' minds as quickly as possible on matters of some moment. With that goal in mind, some boards now begin each meeting with a "president's hour," an opportunity for the chief executive to share with trustees, in executive session, concerns of uppermost importance—the issues, as one trustee stated, "that keep the president awake at night." These are occasions for the president, without others present, to think aloud, seek advice, or alert the board to unanticipated events or problems. At one college, the president's hour takes the form of a breakfast on the first morning of the board meeting—partly social, partly a frank report by the president, and partly a stage setter for the meeting. At another institution, the president's hour is a relaxed and candid after-dinner "fireside chat." Whatever the precise format, the president's hour should *not* be used as a time for the president's report, a routine accounting of the state of the institution or a laundry list of updates, which often is delivered in a public session.

At the fall board meeting of a tuition-dependent college, the president's hour concerned the impact of an unanticipated enrollment shortfall on the current budget year. The president outlined cost-saving strategies that had already been adopted, told the board what was known at that point about the reason for the enrollment decline (an unprecedented decline in freshman-to-sophomore retention), explained how staff proposed to study the factors behind the retention problem, described how the issue was reflected in the agendas of certain key board committees, and invited questions and suggestions from the board. On other occasions, presidents have used the hour to preview alternative structures for a strategic planning process, to discuss the likely effects on public relations and campus morale of the proposed elimination of an academic program and three faculty positions, and to explore openly some tensions among the senior staff.

Most trustees prize the president's hour because these occasions draw board members closer to the inner workings of the institution and of the president's mind. The board has the opportunity to think along with the president about important emergent problems. The president's hour enables trustees to exercise their intellectual muscles and, at the same time, offers the president a private, sympathetic, and secure arena to test ideas and to raise concerns that are difficult to broach elsewhere.

The president's hour requires that the board appreciate the value of questions as well as answers and the identification of the right problems as much as the right solutions. When one president raised a basic question about the tradeoff between quality and quantity in student admissions, one trustee testily replied, "Hey, that's what we pay you to figure out." The president's hour assumes that the president and board are jointly responsible for sound decisions. If the board wants the president to be open and honest, then the trustees should not expect clairvoyance and infallibility.

The Board Chair

The chair quite literally conducts the meeting. As the board's guide, the chair should take a few minutes at the start to outline the agenda, the relationships among issues, the linkages to long-term goals, and any milestones that may have been achieved since the board last met. For example, one chair began a recent meeting with a restatement of the goals that the board had adopted: to rethink financial aid policy, to strengthen the college's relationship to the sponsoring church, and to participate in the development of a campus master plan and long-term capital budget. The chair proceeded to describe briefly the committee agendas in relation to these goals and explain that, after the committees met and reported to the board, all trustees would divide into small groups to reflect on the committees' conclusions and then to report reactions and questions to the full board. As the chair commented later, "I want to make sure each meeting advances the goals we've adopted and that trustees can see that actually happening. I find that because I have to explain at the meeting how all the pieces fit together, I've become much more conscious about how meeting time is structured."

The leadership style of the board chair and committee chairs also influences the quality of trustee participation and the tone of the deliberations. In the name of efficiency, too many chairs rush through agendas and push for premature closure. Others, presumably to be inclusive, allow discussions to proceed aimlessly and endlessly. The board or committee chair should first delineate clear questions and goals to guide the discussion: What are we trying to accomplish? Is our goal to brainstorm, to offer specific advice, or to make a decision? The chair should encourage orderly yet lively participation, clarify trustees' comments and suggestions, and periodically summarize the sense of the group. The chair should also attempt to elicit the comments and viewpoints of more reticent trustees with either a general question to all trustees who have been silent to that point or by a direct invitation to a trustee with expertise or known concerns. As one chair described the role, "I think of myself as a facilitator—not a dictator. I'm trying to get the best out of a whole group of talented people. If folks aren't speaking up, it's my responsibility to make sure they do, even if discussions sometimes get a little hot or drawn out. I want to help the board find common ground, good decisions we all can live with."

Frequently, even engaging and substantive discussions simply end, and neither the board nor the staff understands what should or will occur next. Often nothing does, hardly a surprise under the circumstances. The goal should be to conclude the discussion with a clear articulation, by the chair or sometimes by the president or staff liaison, of who will do what, by when. On important issues of policy and strategy, the chair might ask the appropriate senior officer to recapitulate what he or she takes to be the trustees' "marching orders" and to identify any unresolved "mixed messages" from the trustees. A university board recently adopted a related strategy: a follow-up session at each board meeting where trustee committees and staff report on the status of items, questions, and concerns the board raised at the previous meeting. The impetus for this innovation was the board's realization that, for seven years, trustees and staff had discussed the shortcomings of the administrative technology system, and, despite periodic complaints by trustees and staff, the issue was never settled. Instead, the question would resurface every year or two, only to be neglected or buried again. With the addition of the follow-up session, staff are aware that the board expects and, in fact, demands regular updates until an issue has been satisfactorily resolved.

Staff

The institution's president and the senior staff liaisons to board committees are crucial to productive and successful meetings. Without staff support and involvement, few of the innovations suggested here are likely to be adopted and institutionalized. Likewise, staff with a contempt for trustees can subvert the governance process rather effortlessly, at least for a period of time, by skewing information, withholding knowledge, or monopolizing air time.

The board of trustees has the responsibility to make key decisions. Staff have the information and expertise trustees need to make these decisions. Staff should encourage trustee participation and enhance the board's grasp of complex issues so that the trustees ultimately make better decisions. To serve these purposes, the staff should empower rather than overwhelm the board, facilitate rather than dominate the discussion, and focus rather than divert trustee attention.

The president of one college, where board committees had become passive audiences for staff reports and recommendations, decided that the administration should "report to the board in a 'mix it up' teaching fashion that sustains interest and prompts more trustee involvement and questions." To realize this objective, the president and the staff had to work much more closely with the board and committee chairs to develop agendas and to send concise information, clearly tied to institutional and board goals, well in advance of actual meetings.

Perhaps most significantly, the staff enclosed for each major agenda item a set of proposed discussion questions that were designed to lift the trustees' sights into the realm of policy and strategy and to afford board members the chance to contemplate key aspects of the issues beforehand. At meetings, the questions that had been distributed in advance guided the discussion. For example, discussion questions posed at one college's buildings and grounds committee meeting concerned the implications of the institution's focus on interdisciplinary studies for the design and utilization of a proposed science center. In the course of the discussion, the staff encouraged trustees to explore the consequences of proposals and resisted the temptation to provide the "right" answers or to simplify matters that were, in fact, complicated. Trustee interest and creativity increased markedly as a result of these changes in the staff's procedures and posture.

COMMITTEES AND COMMITTEE STRUCTURES

Most boards depend on standing committees to study issues and make recommendations to the full board. Many trustees go so far as to say that committees do the board's "real work." If so, much of it, unfortunately, entails operations and administration rather than policy and strategy.

Why Committees Underperform

Typically, committees underperform for many of the same reasons boards do: the lack of long-term agendas, reliance on poor or incomplete information, and the failure to distinguish between board-level and operational issues. Therefore, committees can benefit from many of the same approaches that make board meetings more effective: an overview by the committee chair, a strategic focus for discussions, prioritized agendas, consent agendas, and fast feedback.

The structure of committees typically mirrors the institution's organization chart and this, almost by definition, exacerbates the tendency of many boards to focus too much attention on operations. Each committee burrows deeply and narrowly into an administrator's portfolio. "A series of silos" was the image invoked by one trustee.

Inasmuch as the staff liaisons cannot readily invade the territory of other administrators, committees are further constrained and less apt to entertain issues that cross administrative lines. Significant matters such as enrollment management, technology, and marketing fall between the cracks or jurisdictions of the academic affairs, finance, student life, and advancement committees.

On one side of the equation, committees need to feel needed. On the other side, no staff liaison wants to admit that there are too few issues within that individual's domain to warrant a committee meeting at any given time. As a result of these two syndromes, staff continue to develop agendas, and committees continue to meet. With a reciprocal lack of enthusiasm, the staff think, "Here they come again," and the trustees think, "Here we go again."

At worst, standing committees seem to function like a huddle of Monday morning quarterbacks, at best, like a shadow cabinet or a squad of cheerleaders. One administrator described the propensity of staff to deploy committees as champions of a particular perspective, "The name of the game here is, 'My committee is more powerful than your committee, so watch it!'"

Because of the cylindrical and compartmentalized nature of the traditional trustee committee structure, we have observed many occasions on which each of several committees, *unbeknownst* to the others, discussed interrelated aspects of the same strategic problem. However, the entire issue was never considered anywhere within the board's governance structure. For example, at a tuition-dependent college, the issue was five years of enrollment decline. At a single board meeting, the student life committee discussed the effect on retention of conditions in the residence halls; academic affairs looked at trends in applications and enrollment yield; the finance committee considered the budget impact of enrollment declines and increased demand for financial aid; advancement discussed the need to compensate for a budget shortfall through increased annual giving; and buildings and grounds pondered whether an expensive campus beautification program would help the admissions marketing effort.

Each of these discussions touched on an important facet of the problem, but the committee structure (as well the tacit decision *not* to let form follow function in the design of the meeting) provided no opportunity for trustees to discuss the enrollment problem comprehensively. Worse, committees worked at cross purposes: while student affairs concluded that converting double rooms into singles might help retain students, buildings and grounds decided that closing a residence hall would harvest money to beautify the campus.

Restructuring Committee Systems

We already have described some means to alleviate the limitations of committees. Most notably, the board should develop annually a strategic agenda that then enables committees to set "derivative" agendas tightly coupled to institutional priorities. Small-group discussions and plenary sessions also allow trustees to discuss strategic issues that transcend committee boundaries, and staff should always ensure that committee agendas are coordinated.

As helpful as these devices are, boards might consider a more radical but potentially more beneficial alternative: abandon or reconfigure administratively oriented committees. To foreshadow an argument we make at greater length in the next chapter, boards of trustees are quite conservative about self-reform, especially as regards the trustee committee structure. Many, if not most, board members prefer a familiar and tidy system in which each committee has a sharply (and narrowly) defined scope of responsibility. More innovative, more adventurous boards have taken a different tack, however.

The board of a theological school concluded at a retreat that their present committee structure was not likely to contribute to the fulfillment of the institution's strategic plan. Therefore, the trustees decided to revamp the committees to conform to the priorities established by the plan. While the fundraising and finance committees remained intact, others were replaced by committees on globalization of the curriculum, church relations, and continuing education for the ministry—three of the plan's pivotal initiatives.

A less radical measure under consideration at a prestigious women's college will create four councils (business affairs, campus affairs, external affairs, and governance and board affairs) as umbrellas for clusters of standing committees. The council on campus affairs, for example, will oversee the activities and coordinate the annual agendas of the student life, admissions, and trustee-faculty relations committees, which will meet only as necessary. The council chairs will orchestrate the annual agendas of the four councils and suggest strategic issues for in-depth discussion at board meetings.

At another college, the board's "core" committees—finance, academic affairs, and advancement—now meet as "committees of the whole," for between one and four hours, with all members of the board present. The chair of each of these committees still works with the staff to develop the agenda, and the committee chair still leads the meeting, but now the entire board attends and participates. This practice eliminates a major downside of committee systems which, almost unavoidably, present the board with two equally undesirable alternatives: accept committee recommendations with little or no debate, or repeat before the full board the discussion the committee just had. The chair explained the problem and solution for this board:

> The trustees are sharp enough that they started asking questions in the board as a whole that already had been asked at the committee meeting. They weren't micromanaging. These were legitimate policy questions that came up at board meetings because the person wasn't a member of that committee. Now with the committee of the whole structure, all trustees participate directly in the meeting, which enables the entire board to get involved with important issues and to understand better what is going on in key areas of the university.

Even within the constraints of a "normal" standing committee structure, boards should not have to choose either to "rubber stamp" a committee's recommendation or reiterate the entire discussion. The problem can be mitigated to some degree through continuous agendas and derivative work plans for each committee. Committees can report to the board about significant issues on the horizon and seek input well before positions are hardened. Also, committees can "check back" or "touch base" with the board and seek additional feedback before recommendations are formally presented.

Task Forces

Many boards now use task forces—groups commissioned to handle a special assignment and then disband—to replace or supplement standing committees. While trustees accustomed only to standing committees may regard task forces as a major departure from tradition, most boards, in fact, already use ad hoc groups for CEO searches, strategic planning, and capital campaigns, for example. Boards intuitively recognize that certain important, time-sensitive assignments are best delegated to a task force or work group. On college boards, task forces have been established, among other purposes, to study and make recommendations on tuition policy and institutional marketing, to explore the advisability of outsourcing certain services, to evaluate new information technology, to introduce Total Quality Management, and even to undertake a board development effort.

Board members usually relish task forces, which tend to be strategic, results-driven, and timely—a sharp contrast to the tedium and open-endedness trustees associate with standing committees. As a trustee remarked, "The task force helped the board understand the problem and recommend directions. There was a material difference compared to regular committees in the board's sense of ownership. Standing committees are an empty ritual, a burden rather than value added."

Task forces on college governing boards often include faculty, administrators, students, alumni, and community leaders. This creates an opportunity to strengthen relationships with stakeholders and to enlist talented individuals, perhaps without sufficient interest or commitment to warrant an appointment to the board, yet eager to work for a defined period on a specific topic of particular interest.

The Executive Committee

The executive committee—which at many institutions tends to be influential, even hyperactive—deserves particular mention. For reasons discussed in Chapter 3, yet relevant here as well, any device that creates an "inner board" (e.g., those on the executive committee) and an "outer board" (e.g., those with less information and influence) virtually ensures that the board, in toto, will not operate as an effective team. The most constructive roles an executive committee can play are to oversee goal setting and agenda development (i.e., to be a steering committee) and to serve as a preliminary sounding board for the CEO and the board chair. The committee should not, however, as too many do, supplant the board or prejudge issues the board as a whole should decide. One trustee put the matter starkly: "In the past, there was little reason to have a board, since the executive committee decided on everything and just announced its decisions to the others."

Committees That Add Value

No single committee structure will suit every board, for all time. Just as form follows function in good meetings, so should the board's organization reflect institutional purposes. In other words, a board should be organized, to the fullest extent possible, in light of institutional strategy, not in light of organizational structure. In fact, we are tempted to assert that one should be able to infer the institution's strategy from an analysis of the board's committee structure. Committees or task forces on enrollment management, diversity, educational technology, community service, or productivity speak volumes about an institution's concerns and priorities. The typical array of committees (e.g., academic affairs, finance, and physical plant) reveals nothing.

Despite the limitations of standing committees, boards cling to them precisely because the structure seems so immutable. What, trustees wonder, will happen if we eliminate the buildings and grounds or student affairs committee? If the dissolution of the traditional committee system seems too extreme, incremental change may be a better tack. Task forces offer a low-risk way to experiment with strategic committees without abandoning the current structure. Joint committee meetings highlight for trustees the cross-functional nature of strategic issues. And scheduling meetings of standing committees only on an as-needed basis should clarify which committees are really essential and how often each should convene. In the meantime, staff and committee chairs will be spared the need to devise agendas with no strategic significance, and trustees will be spared the need to endure such sessions.

PROVIDING INFORMATION TO GUIDE BOARD DECISION MAKING

The Information Problem

Most trustees complain that the staff provides too much information that communicates too little. Trustees are overwhelmed by the volume of information and shortchanged on the value. Just as architects and designers claim that "less is more," members of effective boards have discovered that succinct information, targeted explicitly on top priorities, improves the caliber of discussion and the quality of decisions.

The information furnished to most boards suffers three flaws. First, the thick pre-meeting packets deal with such a broad range of issues that high priority matters are obscured. One trustee remarked, "Our president has a tendency to paper the board. There's too much stuff, which makes it hard for the typical board member to sort through and see what is important. It is a difficult balance to strike, but you cannot communicate by overcommunicating." Staff realize this too. One senior administrator confessed, "We send the board 'too much, too late.'"

Lawrence Butler argues for a "mission-driven" approach to determine what information a board needs. "For example, a mission that stresses the importance of the 'highest standards of scholarship' may require [board] monitoring and evaluating of faculty's scholarly research and its perceived value in the academic community. One that stresses 'reaching out to the underprivileged' may require the [board] to pay special attention to fund-raising for scholarships and other student support" ("Overhauling" 1995, 32).

The failure to provide this kind of mission-driven information may suggest to some a sinister plot by the staff to overwhelm and confuse the board. That's rarely the case. A surfeit of trivial information more typically indicates that the trustees have not clearly delineated the board's roles and priorities and, therefore, lack the capacity to instruct the staff intelligently about what materials to provide. Without such guidance from the board, most presidents engage, as one trustee posited, "in classic 'cover your tail' behavior. The last thing you want as a president is for the board to blow up and say, 'You never told us what was going on!'"

The second problem is that the information supplied to boards tends to be too operational in nature. To extend Butler's examples, even if a board explicitly identifies the importance of the "highest standards of scholarship" or "reaching out to the underprivileged" as priority areas that require the board's oversight, data that focus on managerial or operational aspects of these issues will be unhelpful and diversionary. Imagine two boards, one with a packet that lists all of the faculty's scholarly publications for the past five years, and the other with a succinct graphic analysis of five-year trends in the faculty's funded research and scholarly output, by department or college. Even if the members of the first board had the patience to sort through so much material, what could they be expected to conclude? Meanwhile, the second board would be primed to have a consequential discussion about the reasons for and significance of changes over time in faculty research productivity.

The third problem is that some trustees receive more information than others. Because so many boards rely so heavily on relatively self-contained standing committees (or the executive committee), most boards have, at once, pockets of deep knowledge and complete ignorance on the same topic. One trustee characterized the confusion: "How does the board communicate with constituents? The student affairs committee spends a lot of time on this, but I don't know that much about it because I'm not on that committee. The board as a whole doesn't do much. I don't know. Maybe the faculty affairs committee does." A board's collective responsibility assumes equal access to information by all trustees, a practice that yields a handsome dividend. As a trustee remarked, "Three or four years ago, this board was just incompetent. It was run by a few people who dictated the decisions. All that has changed. There's a deep commitment to having everyone understand the needs of the institution and engaged in working on them. No one is left out of the loop; everyone gets full information on everything."

Board Books

Nearly all of the information trustees have for board meetings arrives, usually a few days in advance, in a "board book" or "trustee packet." Basically, the book includes the agenda and background materials for the board meeting and for either all of the committee meetings or only the committees on which the recipient serves. It is, almost always, a thick loose-leaf notebook, with tabs and dividers separating the sections.

The most informative and useful board books include some or all of these features:

- a cover memo from the institution's president and/or the board chair that outlines significant developments since the previous meeting and previews the goals and key issues for this meeting

- agendas for all committee meetings and the board meeting that include for each major item a set of discussion questions, a concise statement as to why the matter must come before the board, and essential supporting materials
- an executive summary of any document in the book longer than a few pages
- minutes of the previous meetings of the board and committees.
- a list of the board's current goals
- a copy of the mission statement and/or a list of principal goals from the strategic plan
- evaluation forms for board and committee meetings
- a roster of trustees and staff, with addresses, phone and fax numbers, and committee assignments

Comprehensiveness does not mean that the board book must be voluminous. Trustees are much more apt to prepare for meetings if the staff: (1) provides succinct and, wherever possible, graphic information that illuminates the issues to be discussed; (2) mails the board books in time to arrive at least a week or 10 days in advance; and (3) does not distribute and discuss materials on site that trustees have not had a chance to read or absorb.

It is difficult, as this trustee notes, to overstate the importance of focused, timely information to guide deliberation and decision making: "We've really improved the quality of our discussions by improving the quality of material the staff provides for board meetings. The quality of the executive summaries is excellent. We want to have the best, most appropriate information in order to make intelligent decisions."

Interim Communications

While board books are vital, effective boards also rely on regular communications from the president and sometimes the chair to stay apprised of institutional affairs. One president sends articles, from time to time, about the institution and higher education more generally, usually selectively underlined and annotated to establish the connection to particularly salient issues on campus. For example, one mailing included an article about tuition increases in private colleges photocopied from the *Chronicle of Higher Education*. The president circled the national average and wrote in the margin, "Our increase this year was 1% less." Trustees thus had a very quick lesson on national tuition trends, along with important information on where this college fit in the larger picture. Over time, such knowledge accumulates and permits better board discussions and decisions.

Another president sends a monthly update to all trustees on campus events, actions taken as a result of the last board meeting, and even personal milestones in the lives of board members. A recent memo included a progress report on the capital campaign, the college's response to a major alcohol policy violation at a fraternity, and news that a trustee's mother had died. A trustee commented, "I live far from campus, and I'm a busy person. Frankly, without being reminded, I don't wake up every day thinking about the college. Getting these little memos from the president really helps."

CONCLUSION

Consultant Mitchell Nash (Dressler 1995) asserted that the most common complaints about meetings in the workplace are:

- the purpose of the meeting is unclear
- the meeting participants are unprepared
- key people are absent or late
- the conversation veers off track
- participants don't discuss issues; they dominate the conversation, argue, or take no part at all
- decisions made at the meeting are not followed up

In their roles as managers of businesses, trustees are understandably appalled at such wastefulness and rightfully insistent that the return on meetings justify the time and resources expended. Why do these same individuals assume that board meetings for nonprofit institutions should be any less productive?

Keys to effective board meetings include: agendas and practices that reflect and bolster institutional strategy, structures that support consequential work, effective leadership, and timely and pertinent information. In many ways, the ingredients of a successful board meeting and a first-rate graduate student seminar are not very different: clear learning objectives, relevant readings, meaningful assignments, a supportive environment, skillful facilitation, opportunities for participants to lead as well as listen, and an open-minded search for consensus, conflict, and defensible conclusions.

NOTE

1. In those few instances in which a board meets very infrequently or for very short periods, and has no intention to do otherwise, the trustees should soberly consider the most vital tasks to accomplish in the time available. One board, which meets for approximately 18 hours a year, has tentatively concluded that, beyond the discharge of basic fiduciary responsibilities, the board would do best to "decide what matters most to the college's future and to monitor progress in those areas." Whether that can be accomplished in so little time remains to be seen.

CHAPTER 6

Understanding and Responding to Resistance

THE RIDDLE

I f the vast majority of trustees and CEOs were favorably inclined toward board development, the task would be relatively simple. Reality, however, suggests otherwise. Board development falters far more often from a lack of political will than from a lack of practical solutions.

In truth, relatively few institutions commit much "hard currency" in the form of time, money, and effort to board development. Thus, the riddle arises: If boards of trustees are so vital to institutional success, why is methodical attention to board development the exception and not the rule? In other words, why does board development engender deep-seated doubts and strong opposition among some trustees and some CEOs? Based on interviews and conversations with hundreds of board members and campus CEOs, we have identified six reasons, three from the viewpoint of trustees and three from the perspective of presidents.

The main purpose of this chapter is to state and then rebut the arguments against board development. It is essential to remember that the positions against board development that follow were constructed from the words of board members and CEOs (verbatim quotes are so noted). In effect, each numbered argument represents a composite statement, based on the criticism of opponents to board development. These are *not* the words or views of the authors, whereas the rebuttals are, unless otherwise noted.

Although we have structured most of the chapter as a dialectic or point-counterpoint, this is not just an intellectual exercise. In order to minimize opposition to board development, proponents of the process must understand the mindset and apprehensions of the resisters. Likewise, trustees and CEOs eager to advocate and implement board development must grasp the most persuasive arguments to counter and allay detractors' concerns. We deal first with the reasons some trustees resist, and then consider parallel themes that account for resistance among CEOs.

RESISTANCE TO BOARD DEVELOPMENT

The Trustees' Perspective: Argument 1

Position

There is no conclusive evidence that sustained, systematic attention to board development is a promising and efficient path to improving institutional performance. If there were such evidence, more institutions would undertake board development in order to gain a strategic advantage over the competition. Furthermore, if this tactic worked, the successes would be conspicuous and widely imitated. In fact, however, cause-and-effect links between outstanding boards and outstanding institutions have not been convincingly established. It is not as if the best nonprofits have the best boards and vice versa.

> Let me give you an example. ——— College, not far from here, has no debt, no enrollment problems. That board doesn't know anything. The president is a prima donna; he's running the show by himself. He showers the board with perquisites. There's bonding, golfing, and chances to introduce your wives to one another. As long as the college is running well, who cares how the board is operating. . . . It works for them, but [researchers] would probably tell them that they're a terrible board. Meanwhile, the college is in great shape.

The relationship between a board's performance and an institution's effectiveness seems tenuous at best. Many prestigious colleges and universities, for instance, have long abided marginally effective, largely ceremonial boards. Unless and until persuasive evidence can be marshalled to establish that the development of an effective board is tantamount to the development of an effective institution, why bother?

Counterargument

Research that we conducted on the effectiveness of college and university boards (Holland, Chait, and Taylor 1989) did, in fact, demonstrate a positive and systematic association between board performance, as measured by interviewer-rated competencies and trustee self-assessments, and institutional success, as measured by five-year trends on financial reserves, net student revenues, institutional wealth, and academic emphasis. Further support for a positive association derives from a recent analysis of the financial performance of 24 companies that were the weakest stocks in the portfolio of the California

Public Employees Retirement Systems (CALPERS) in 1990. For the five previous years, these companies lagged the S&P 500 Index by an average of 86 percentage points. After CALPERS pressured the directors and managers to improve, these same corporations each exceeded the Index by an average of 109 percentage points (Minow 1994). Taken together, these results suggest that governance does make a difference.

Even if this were not the case, one should not conclude that no relationship exists between board performance and institutional performance. Quite possibly, the linkages are more subtle: a competent board at a college has a positive effect on the president, the president on the faculty, and the faculty on the students. There are multiple actors linked by complex interactions that produce multiple effects, all difficult to measure.

The greater the distance between an individual or a group and a college's end product (e.g., the discovery and transmission of knowledge), the more difficult it is to establish causality. Hence, incontrovertible proof of causality may be an unreasonable standard to apply. If student learning, for example, were accepted as an important barometer of institutional success, it would be comparatively easy to argue, though still hard to prove, that faculty "cause" student learning and hence institutional success. The argument becomes more tenuous for people further removed from the process, such as deans, registrars, groundskeepers, and perhaps even presidents. There is little conclusive cause-and-effect evidence about most aspects of institutional performance, as reflected by conventional academic and financial yardsticks. Of greater relevance here, however, is the recognition that the difficulty of demonstrating a valid connection empirically should be viewed as a conceptual and methodological problem rather than as *prima facie* evidence that no connection exists.

In many respects, the argument against board development turns significantly on the definitions of institutional performance. Even if one accepts the conventional definition of success as goal achievement, questions still arise about *which* goals to include. Is an attractive campus a measure of sound institutional performance? If so, then groundskeepers probably are crucial to the college's success. The attainment of other goals can be traced more directly to the board's actions, such as the completion of a capital campaign, improved community relations, or the retention of a talented president.

Finally, trustees skeptical about the actual value of board development overlook its *symbolic* value as an expression of a commitment, at the top of the organizational pyramid, to professional development, continuous quality improvement, and a learning organization, concepts that are associated with successful enterprises. As we emphasized in Chapter 1, boards add value whenever they model the behaviors that they want their institutions to manifest. Here is an opportunity to do just that.

The Trustees' Perspective: Argument 2

Position

The best ways for a nonprofit board to serve and improve the institution is to attend to the "bottom line" and to evaluate the CEO. Board members have a limited amount of time to devote to trusteeship. If a board is going to make a difference, surely it will be in those areas that most directly affect the bottom line, such as budgeting and finance, fundraising, physical plant, and endowment management.

Most trustees know how to run a business and how to run it well. This is where board members can add value. In the case of colleges and universities, higher education can be seen as simply another industry: "A university must be run like a complex business." By comparison, few college trustees have sophisticated knowledge of teaching, learning, and research. Thus, one college trustee asserted:

> A board has only two roles: to hire and fire the president and to build a network to raise money. The other committees, like education and student affairs, are really there just for a gut check. Otherwise, we don't bring a lot to the table.

The president's performance is the best measure that lay trustees have for evaluating institutional effectiveness, and board members do know how to evaluate a CEO. Trustees could double or triple the amount of time they devote to the college and still not understand fully the operations of the institution or the larger context: "There aren't four people on the board who understand the bylaws or four who can quote our mission. There's just too much for people to absorb. Things move too fast to keep everybody up to date. That would require full-time devotion." It makes much more sense, therefore, for the board to concentrate on the president's performance.

Given limited time and limited knowledge, how could a board of trustees, in good conscience, divert time from urgent matters of a business nature in order to indulge in board development and concepts as soft and vague as group dynamics, socialization, and self-reflection? A board of trustees would have to be almost irresponsible to pursue the uncertain payoffs of board development to the neglect of its fiduciary responsibility for the college's finances and leadership. Faculties can fiddle while Rome burns, boards cannot.

Board development is a self-indulgent and vain artifact of a narcissistic generation; a process that rarely, if ever, affects institutional performance: "Most of our trustees think of it as navel-gazing," commented a university president. The $10,000 to $20,000 cost of a retreat with a facilitator is a questionable use of institutional resources, especially in a period of financial hardship.

Counterargument

This argument rests upon a false dichotomy: that board development and activities that affect the bottom line are in conflict. Board development is not about "touchy-feely" parlor games. At its best, it conveys information crucial to responsible governance in areas such as finance, fundraising, professional norms, the content of programs, measures of quality, and the nature and limits of authority in nonprofit organizations. Far from distracting trustees from their "real work," such learning enables boards to capably exercise institutional oversight.

Most college and university trustees are not experts in higher education. To oversee the "business" effectively, board members need to understand what the college produces and how the production process operates. Otherwise, disaster may strike.

> We were all pretty naive about how a college ran and what we should do. We didn't really understand the finances of our own institution. . . . We didn't realize that more students meant more debt because we were providing such a subsidy. . . . This illustrates one of the darkest hours of the board, and it was under my chairmanship. It happened because we didn't know the facts of life and we didn't have a sense of the board's collective responsibility for the institution. We had a hard time getting the board to even look at it.

This board subsequently launched an extensive series of education hours for trustees that "have been especially useful in helping the board learn things we needed to know *in order to carry out our role more effectively*" (emphasis added).

Even topics like "group dynamics" and "socialization" have their place. Boards are peculiar organizations—corporate units composed of individual achievers. In order to make collective decisions, trustees must know one another well enough to work together compatibly. Social interaction promotes camaraderie, accentuates inclusion, and increases trustee satisfaction. In turn, these positive sentiments and experiences strengthen the trustees' moral and financial commitment to the board and to the institution.

Most trustees will be enthusiastic about board development as long as the process elevates the board's ability to govern. In other words, there must be a tangible, direct connection between board development and the effective discharge of trustee responsibilities. For instance, board members almost invariably regard retreats, president's hours, and educational sessions as more valuable than ordinary board meetings precisely because these alternative formats enable trustees to understand, discuss, and shape strategic policies and priorities. In short, these devices equip boards to govern better.

The Trustees' Perspective: Argument 3

Position

There are no great boards, only boards with some great trustees. Better to appoint as trustees a few superstars than try to develop the board as a whole. The best institutions do not achieve distinction primarily, or even largely, as the result of brilliant governance by the board of trustees as a whole. A few exceptional trustees, not the board, make the difference.

> You only need a small team, not a herd. Get a few good players, train them well, and keep them focused on a few top-priority issues.

> We have a hunt club in town that's limited to 40 people. That's where things get done for this college. That's how decisions get made.

> Eight, nine, ten people have been the key. It's always that way.

Realistically, boards are too large, too intermittently assembled, and too uneven in quality to be effective as an entity. The size of the board, typically 20 or 25 members (and sometimes far more), and the infrequency of meetings, 3 or 4 times a year for a day (and sometimes much less), militate against collective competency. Boards cannot congeal as a team under these circumstances. The trustees, to be honest, do well to remember one another's names and to track the course of issues from one meeting to the next.

As large as these logistical obstacles loom, the greater barrier, by far, concerns the inherent limitations of individual board members. Trustees are appointed for sundry reasons—affluence, social and denominational affiliations, demography, geography, and popularity, to name a few. Intellectual horsepower and analytical astuteness are not always prerequisites. The harsh reality is that a board of trustees is, at best, a mixed bag of abilities and personalities. Sometimes the tasks associated with the governance of a complex organization, such as a college or university, are simply too great for their talents. The average trustee is, well, average.

Even in those instances where board members are intellectually equal to the task, eccentric personalities and individual biases commonly interfere with the board's overall effectiveness. Some trustees are surly and others are disingenuous. Some attempt to dominate while others attempt to manipulate. Some are obsessed with athletics, others with fraternities. Thus, the "real" leaders of the board must repeatedly rise above the liabilities of the rest.

> What's the most important lesson about improving board performance? Don't ask more of people than they can give. Human beings have strengths and limitations, so you have to accommodate to that reality . . . I'll never get over the disappointment about the limitations of some people. It will be a lifetime struggle for me to come to terms with that reality. That's a lesson and a continuing frustration for me.

Rotating committee membership has helped, but it's not enough. There still are incompetent people who will never be able to do the job. We need more really capable people on this board.

What makes a board effective? Select people who are well qualified already and who have the skills and capacities that are needed by the college.

If the basic capacities are not there, you can't create them. You need people with some vision and leadership skills to build on.

In the end, it is far more efficacious to recruit and retain a few extraordinary trustees than to endeavor, through board development, to overcome the deficiencies of many mediocre ones.

Counterargument

From the Trustee Demonstration Project and various consultancies, we have identified three different types of boards: communitarian, oligarchic, and auxiliary. The key elements of each type are outlined in Exhibit 6.1 (an extended analysis of this typology is forthcoming). We wish here only to highlight that the communitarian boards are the most inclusive and attempt to match each trustee's talents to the institution's needs. Explained a trustee on one such board, "You have to work your way *out* of the group. Our obligation is to help you become a contributing member of the group, and we've failed if we haven't recognized and used your potential." On the oligarchic board, trustees, as one noted, have to earn their way *into* the group; "The board is dominated by a bunch of big-city lawyers who don't exactly give the rest of us the key to the inner sanctum of the board." And on auxiliary boards, trustees are "on call"; that is, the institution's head (usually the president) decides if and when to include and utilize various members. "You have to treat the board as a class," a college CEO asserted. "It's a teaching job. My job is to teach them trusteeship. . . . I've had to hold the board and faculty apart until each knows enough about the other to have a productive dialog. They're ready now."

Of immediate relevance, the communitarian boards had the highest interview scores on five of the six competencies (slightly lower on the political dimension) at the start of the project and the highest interview scores on all six competencies at the end of the project (see Exhibit 1.1 for an outline of competencies). In other words, the boards most disposed to be inclusive were also the most competent across all six dimensions of effective trusteeship, and not, as might be expected, only on the interpersonal dimension.

Small boards are not an inherent problem. Indeed, many trustees on comparatively small boards, such as Dartmouth College (16 members) and the President and Fellows of Harvard College (9 members, including four institu-

Types of Boards

	Communitarian	Oligarchic	Auxiliary
Allegiance	Core values of the institution	Institutional survival	Office of the CEO
Mindset	Let's find and solve problems together	A few of us know what to do and how to do it	What does the CEO want to do and how can I help?
Group Dynamics	Have to work your way out of the group	Have to work your way into the group	CEO determines the group(s)
Involvement	Involve everyone, match talents to needs	Race belongs to the swiftest; power blocs compete	Task-specific as "anointed" by the CEO
Power	Broadly distributed, empowered by group	Vigilantism, empowered by inner circle	Reflected power from CEO, trustees are spear carriers
Decision Making	Consultative and consensual	Prescriptive and competitive	Rubber stamp, adopt directives
Board-President Relationship	Partners, mutual capacity to influence	CEO works for board; CEO proposes, board decides	Board works for CEO; CEO declares, board affirms
Evaluation of Board	Self-reflection and evaluation by entire board	Self-evident from institutional success	CEO provides informal feedback to board

EXHIBIT 6.1

tional officers), report that the board's small size enables robust discussion, broad participation, and camaraderie. Complications arise when a small group controls and thereby alienates the other members of a large board. Complained one marginalized trustee, "Decisions are being made on the golf course and in country clubs. People are losing interest in participating. Some people feel excluded, and these people are reluctant to vocalize their concerns." The issue is not whether to have an inner circle so much as why an inner circle requires an outer circle. If the answer is "money," then one must ask why anyone would find "affluence without influence" to be an attractive arrangement and why, more generally, the members of the outer circle would be motivated to perform devotedly.

Most trustees on college boards care deeply about the institution or at least about higher education more generally (Taylor, Chait, and Holland 1991). Afforded the opportunity to learn and participate, most will do so. Few want to occupy a seat at the table silently. When trustees behave as if governance were a low priority, very often the root cause can be traced to the fact that these individuals were deliberately confined to the periphery of major policy and strategy questions. If trustees feel out of the loop, uneducated about the institution, and marginalized, then these board members will almost certainly be apathetic and disengaged. The stakes are too low to spark inspired performance. On the other hand, when such board members are educated, informed, and involved in issues central to the institution, they are far more likely to commit greater energy and extra effort to trusteeship.

When dispirited trustees lament, "I was a voice in the wilderness," or "I was superfluous," that does not signify irresponsible behavior on the part of a board member or substantiate the folly of collective action as an ideal. More likely, these trustees mean exactly what they said. They *were* voices in the wilderness; they *were* superfluous. Proponents of the inner circle school of boardsmanship cannot simultaneously contend that most trustees, as a matter of necessity, must passively support the brain trust of the board and the CEO of the institution, and then bristle when the board as a whole underperforms or when individual trustees withdraw psychologically or resign altogether.

The Presidents' Perspective: Argument 1

Position

There is scant hard evidence that indicates that board development leads to effective boards and then to effective institutions. It is difficult, if not impossible, in a complex institution to determine a clear cause-and-effect relationship between acts of leadership and institutional outcomes. In a large black box that encompasses all of the ground between inputs and outputs, causality becomes virtually obscured. In studies of colleges and universities, some scholars even question whether presidents exert significant influence over institutional events and subsequent results (Cohen and March 1974; Birnbaum 1988 and 1992). If there are doubts about whether the president has any impact, then one must really question whether boards can have a tangible positive effect on outcomes, aside from financial support. "We must wait a long time for any payoff from board development, and in the meantime, we don't want to alienate the donors," explained a university president.

It would be impolitic and probably self-destructive to confess publicly to this doubt; better and more prudent to treat the board of trustees like a roof, but speak to and of its members as if they were the institution's foundation. It is vitally important to have a roof in order to protect a house from the ravages of the external environment. To fulfill that basic purpose effectively typically requires little maintenance and minor attention. If, from time to time, the roof springs a leak, then the owner makes the necessary repairs, but from a cost-benefit standpoint, it makes little sense to have a state-of-the-art roof. A board is *not* like the faculty, staff, or the student body, which are more akin to electrical, plumbing, and heating and air conditioning systems—truly vital, dynamic units where breakdowns are costly and where the very best equipment can provide tangible advantages.

> What's the most important lesson I've learned about improving the board's performance? Well, I'm very tempted to say that you should just save your energy. Developing a board is very, very hard work, extremely time consuming. I wonder sometimes, why bother? Leave them alone and invest my time in more important things that will pay off for the institution. Bringing about change on a board takes lots of time that could be used more efficiently elsewhere.

The clever CEO devotes just enough attention to the board to ensure that it does not become a major problem. No executive wants the roof to fall in. Thus, the CEO practices preventive maintenance. "Each board meeting is an exercise in damage control," confessed one university president. From that vantage point, the CEO sees the downside of board development far more clearly than the upside: "Between the problem (a so-so board) and the solution (board development), the problem may look better to some of my fellow college presidents."

The key for the CEO is to avoid a board crisis, i.e., having the roof blow off, and to make sure that small leaks are patched quickly so as to prevent major damage. This is done by periodically inspecting the roof and repairing or replacing a shingle here and a shingle there; that is to say, by humoring individual trustees, attending to their particular concerns, adapting to their idiosyncracies and, when necessary, inducing a few changes in the composition of the board.

Individual board members are helpful as sources of advice and expertise, and a small group, like the executive committee, can be a useful "kitchen cabinet." However, power is a zero-sum game. As the board becomes more energized, the CEO becomes less powerful. This is as true for nonprofit organizations as it is for corporations. "Traditionally, corporate leaders have considered a powerful, active board to be a nuisance at best and a force that could improperly interfere in the management of the company at worst. They have preferred directors who are content to offer counsel when asked and to support management in times of crisis" (Lorsch 1995, 107).

Counterargument

Even for a president, institutional effectiveness may not be the sole or best test of the value of board development. Self-preservation may be a better barometer. If so, presidents skeptical about board development should heed the counsel offered to CEOs by an expert on corporate governance: "Chief executives who resist empowered boards must change their attitude. If they do not, they . . . will be the losers because the empowered board is here to stay" (Lorsch 1995, 107).

From an equally pragmatic perspective, a cohesive, committed, and enlightened board poses *less* of a threat to a CEO than a splintered, peripheral, and ignorant board. A trustee warned:

> If the president won't involve the board, then trustees won't have a clue about what is going on, and they won't own the institution. And when a problem arises, and it will, and the CEO needs the trustees, they won't be there. The board won't feel they own the problem, and they won't be willing to solve it.

In the same vein, the CEO of one project site advised:

> Any president who does not see that an active, well-informed board is not a benefit is being extraordinarily short-sighted. You might be able to fend off and hold the board at arm's length for a short period of time, but eventually something will happen that will upset them. And they won't have the context to understand the institution or your leadership style, and then you are playing with dynamite and you are going to get blown out.
>
> On the other hand, if you have a group of trustees that understands the goals of the institution, is very much involved, and appreciates the difficulties of academic administration, they will be more supportive. But they're only going to understand all this by living through some things. You can't throw them the big grenade if they have no backdrop for understanding and then think that they're not going to get shrapnel all over themselves and all over you in the process. You have to spend time on board development, but it's worth it, even if you are only being selfishly pragmatic.

Almost all college trustees recognize that higher education faces formidable challenges and, due mainly to the reform of corporate governance, most realize that a "good" board is supposed to be active. In an effort to be active, less developed boards become still more unpredictable. Without cohesiveness, a shared concept of the board's role, and a common vision for the institution, the actions of individual trustees assume disproportionate significance and, as noted in Chapter 1, sometimes conflict with one another. In the name of active trusteeship, these board members often make special demands for information, intrude on management, and otherwise make a president's lot difficult. Furthermore, when trustees conclude that the president exercises too much control or that the president has withheld or distorted vital information, the activists may move outside legitimate, established channels. "I coveted the opportunity to work with the faculty, but the president had held us apart. I had to be the board-faculty matchmaker when the faculty's relationship with the last president fell apart. I had to go offline and be inappropriate." Even worse, the self-appointed posse may decide, often quite abruptly, that the president must go. (See Chapter 3 for an example.)

Most college presidents want a board to perform certain critical functions: raise money, provide financial stewardship, represent the institution, support the president publicly. A president averse to genuine, substantive involvement by the board runs the risk that there will be too few committed and knowledgeable trustees to perform these valued functions proficiently when the need arises. "If I could do it again," admitted one president, initially a bit dubious about the project,

> I'd have spent more time getting the trustees to talk about their collective values rather than hitting them with specific issues. I'd have learned more about trusteeship, and I wouldn't have assumed that they knew anything about being trustees. The first consultants I hired were for finance and fundraising, and I put trusteeship on the back burner. I'd have been better off bringing in consultants who knew about boards.

Most trustees are not easily fooled. If they are being humored, diverted, or relegated to honorific roles, they know it. They may continue to attend board and committee meetings and to participate as perfunctorily as the president's treatment seems to warrant, but most will not go the extra mile to land a major gift, to publicly defend the president's cutbacks, to expend a precious chit with the governor on the university's behalf, or to mull just a little longer and a little harder over a vexatious issue before the board. An incumbent president asked rhetorically,

> Why should a president put so much effort into board development? For a couple of reasons. In the long run, it makes the president's job easier. Done well, it gives you the support group you can count on in any situation. Second, you get some heavyweight, strong institutional advocates. . . . The university has become an important part of their lives and they're talking it up in key places. So it's worth the energy. All this effort has turned loose a lot of very influential ambassadors.

The CEO's influence over the character and caliber of a corporate board has been well established. Conventional wisdom holds that ". . . over time, chief executives get the boards they want" (Patton and Baker 1987, 12). Because of their pivotal role in board development, college presidents may get the boards they *deserve*, even though campus CEOs, especially in the public sector, do not hold as much sway over their boards as their for-profit counterparts.

The Presidents' Perspective: Argument 2

Position

A little bit of knowlegdge is a dangerous thing for a board of trustees. An informed board can be dangerous and dysfunctional. A board that knows "just enough" might meddle and micromanage. A board that knows "too much" might actually initiate proposals, policies, and strategies. In either case, faculty and staff, concerned that the board has encroached on hallowed turf and trampled professional prerogatives, will exert pressure to restrain the board or otherwise be viewed by key campus constituents as "weak." On the other hand, efforts to bridle the board carry obvious risks. Rather than be caught in this vise, the institution's best interests will be served by crafting a board that asks interesting questions but lacks the knowledge to supply or assess the answers.

For the board to be truly effective, trustees need to have an intimate knowledge of the institution which would necessitate an immersion in learning that few trustees, if any, are prepared to undertake. As even a board chair conceded, "Given the turnover on the board and the trustees' mindset, there's no way to get all of them up to speed on all the issues and problems that we have to consider." In addition, an initiative to better educate board members can trigger impulses that are ill-advised. "Trustees want to spend 50% of their time paddling around campus getting to know faculty and students. They need to know the programs."

If trustee activity were to increase due to board development while, at the same time, the board's knowledge level remained roughly constant, the likelihood of error would increase, quite logically, because the opportunities to act or decide have increased. Rather than court such risks, the board's knowledge should be maintained at a subsistence level: enough to get through one meeting and ready for the next.

Quite simply, the game is not worth the candle. A board development process could spawn an aggressive, assertive board, thereby eroding the president's stature and fraying constituent relations. Better to let sleeping dogs lie.

Counterargument

Ignorance is much more dangerous than knowledge. In reality, educated boards are far less likely than uninformed ones to interfere inappropriately or to act on the basis of incomplete information. Most often, the lack of knowledge and the absence of context curtail the board's capacity to see, much less comprehend, the larger picture. Museum-goers who are knowledgeable about pointillism stand at some distance to appreciate the entire tableau; dilettantes are first drawn close to examine the tiny details because they do not know better.

> The most important change that I've noticed as president has been the board's ability to recognize the difference between policy and management.... Many of the trustees felt like fools when they realized, under the previous president, that while they watched the details, the big picture passed them by.

> Something we are *not* doing now that we did in the past is to allow board discussions to wander around all over the issues and not get straight to the core question.

An enlightened, empowered board does not mean an intrusive, hyperactive board; quite the opposite.

In order to provide intelligent and appropriate oversight, trustees need not be immersed in the institution. Managers, not governors, require intimate knowledge. For any institution at any point in time, there are a limited number of critical performance factors that will spell the difference between success and failure. When a board and an administration together identify these priorities, establish norms, and monitor progress, the board's involvement will almost certainly be channeled toward issues critical to the institution's vitality. At the same time, the process of delimiting these areas serves two important purposes: (1) to make clear to the board that operational matters are usually off limits or occasionally worth only momentary consideration; and (2) to provide the CEO with a board-sanctioned framework to withstand requests by individual trustees for information or actions that lie outside the scope of legitimate board involvement.

There was, for many years, an adage popular among college presidents that always elicited a chuckle among the cognoscente: "Treat the board like mushrooms. Keep them in the dark, covered with dirt, and cut their heads off when they pop up." This aphorism offers dangerous advice. The most damage occurs to presidents and institutions when their boards operate in the dark.

The Presidents' Perspective: Argument 3

Position

It is all but impossible to match trustee talents to institutional needs. CEOs have little or no influence over trustee appointments to public boards and modest leverage, at best, over appointments to private boards. Since the president does not chose the team, trustees' talents and interests do not always match the institution's true needs. Still worse, the trustees may be neither talented nor interested.

To compound the trustee selection problem, no one can be quite sure what decisions will prove to be significant over the long run, a reality that severely limits the institution's ability to match trustee expertise with organizational priorities. There can be a substantial lag time before the positive or negative

consequences of decisions (or inaction) materialize. This situation simultaneously reduces the trustees' impact and relieves the pressure on the board to
be accountable. It is almost impossible for a president or a board to see what
lies ahead over the next 6–12 months (otherwise, boards could develop annual
work plans effortlessly), let alone over the next 3–5 years. On a college board,
what seems significant now—a contract with a vendor, a new compensation
policy, a tempest in an academic department, the sale of property, the installation of condom machines—may scarcely matter later. Conversely, what gar-
ners little attention at the moment—the advent of commercial competition,
or the onset of the "virtual campus"—may loom large later. Under these
circumstances, how can anyone foresee the talents and perspectives that will
be required of a board of trustees?

To make matters still worse, it is difficult to keep score in academe; it is hard
to chart progress. What is measurable (e.g., library utilization) is often relatively unimportant and what is important (e.g., student learning gains) is often
not readily measurable.

Given these conditions, presidents, despite the best of intentions, are at a
loss to determine where trustee attention might be usefully directed or which
levers for change the board might profitably manipulate. If the CEO cannot
select the players, if trustees are not well suited to the game, if the nature of the
game is constantly changing in unpredictable ways, and if disagreements
persist about how the institution should keep score, what can a college
president reasonably expect of a board? Probably not much. Rather than
invest heavily in board development, better to keep one's own expectations,
and those of the board, appropriately low. No one expects a lot from a roof.

Counterargument

Few trustees are any more ordinary than their presidents. To the contrary,
many colleges, some hardly known 100 miles from the campus, count among
their trustees executives of large corporations, partners in major professional
firms, and other conspicuously successful individuals. The fact that most board
members are neither handpicked by the CEO nor experts in higher education
does not mean that trustees are without talent and interest. A lack of
knowledge about the "industry" does not equate to a lack of analytical skills.
Trustees are eminently educable, and colleges and universities purportedly
excel at education. Board development offers the means to further cultivate
the trustees' intellectual assets so as to benefit the institution.

Granted, no one can predict the future with precision. However, the
greatest vulnerability exists in organizations where the CEOs are most insular.
Perhaps more threats and crises, presumably unpredictable, could be averted if
presidents conferred more sincerely with the board, which often has diverse
knowledge and an expansive external perspective. The very fact that the

future cannot be foretold argues for greater, not lesser, trustee involvement in shaping a vision and setting goals. As the trustees' portfolio dovetails with institutional priorities, the stakes rise and board development becomes more imperative.

THE PROOF IS IN THE PUDDING

The arguments against board development should not be lightly dismissed; each has some validity. On the other hand, we believe that the case for board development has greater force, a contention supported by the scores from interviews at the outset and the conclusion of the demonstration project. Overall competency increased 33%, on average, with more dramatic gains in the areas where boards focused the most attention, namely, the educational dimension (42%) and the interpersonal dimension (111%). Only scores on the political dimension decreased (6%).

In the last analysis, however, decisions about whether to initiate, expand, and sustain board development will be based on the tangible, practical benefits as determined by the participants in the process—not by the contours of a philosophical debate or the research of academicians. Since the "testimony" of the participants carries such great weight, we conclude this section of the chapter with representative observations from the trustees and presidents at project sites about the payoffs from board development. The excerpts address not so much the value of specific tools and techniques covered elsewhere in the book (e.g., consent agendas, president's hours, retreats, trustee mentors, and orientation programs) as the more fundamental changes that occurred as a result of taking these steps. The quotations are all trustee responses to this question: "What are the most important changes that you have seen in the way this board operates?"

> The board began to think about itself, its role and functioning, to look purposively at what we do, and how we do business.

> The board is less perfunctory. We've made a concerted effort to be more issues oriented, more policy oriented, less operational, more inclusive.

> The board is more flexible, more aware of its goals as a board.

> It's a more cohesive board, more comfortable with one another than in the past. We think more strategically than we used to.

> The board is more inclusive and focused. The major issues are better integrated now, and will be even more as the core committees meet as committees of the whole.

> We are more disciplined, self-reflective, structured, and intentional.

Board meetings are more focused on the issues. . . . The environment for openness has been introduced. There is a greater ability for interchange among board members and between trustees and the staff.

The board has become much more conscientious and attentive to itself as a board as opposed to simply coming and being stewards for the institution. . . . We spend more time on more things that matter and less time on things that are not important.

FLYING INTO THE HEADWINDS

We started this book with an admonition: that to be truly effective, boards would have to continuously swim against the tide. We want to end on a similar note—not to be somber or bleak, but to underscore the need for *persistence* on the part of trustees and presidents who have resolved, as those at the demonstration sites did, to create boards that add value to their institutions. Pitted against this determination to proceed with board development are the very powerful headwinds of complacency and conservatism.

Fighting Complacency

"We're okay as an institution. There's no crisis. Why tamper with the board?" These comments, offered by a thoughtful board chairman, are quite characteristic of college (and other nonprofit) trustees. Similar sentiments were undoubtedly expressed at various times by board members of Apple, Digital Equipment, General Motors, IBM, K-Mart, Kodak, Sears, Westinghouse, and dozens of other "blue chip" companies that once seemed invulnerable. Smugness can be hazardous and even fatal, as various airlines, department stores, computer companies, and automobile manufacturers learned all too well. Remember Pan American, B. Altman, Wang, and American Motors?

Self-satisfaction can easily be reinforced by self-delusion. We have accumulated considerable data over the past decade that demonstrate that boards of trustees, especially the less effective ones, tend to overestimate their own performance (Holland 1991, 34). In a review of self-assessments by 1,128 trustees of a diverse sample of 61 college boards, there was extremely small variability across sites or across the performance criteria at any single site (Chait and Taylor 1987). Virtually every board was rated above average by every trustee. Yet, ample evidence exists that board performance varies widely among organizations (Taylor 1987). Likewise, among the Trustee Demonstration Project sites, the self-assessments by boards were, without exception, more generous than the scores assigned by the researchers based on evaluations of the interview transcripts.

Another form of self-deception occurs when trustees confuse institutional success with board effectiveness. At a college, as long as enrollments are robust and the finances are solid, the board may be content to travel on cruise control. "Being on a board is like being in the army. There are long stretches of boredom followed by crises where you have to act fast and effectively." On one campus where the institution was recently ranked among the very best of a certain category by a national guide, the trustees were self-congratulatory. Yet, the board meets, on average, 18–20 hours a year and rarely grapples with pivotal questions of policy and strategy. If the college dropped from first to tenth, would the board also assume responsibility for the decline and behave differently? Have the trustees considered the possibilities to further outpace the competition or to further secure the college's status that have not been realized due to the board's mediocre performance? Probably not. A board's principal role is *not* to stand by until the fire alarm sounds. The board's goal should be to improve decision making, "to decrease the possibility of mistakes and to increase the speed with which they are corrected" (Pound 1995, 94).

Resisting Conservatism

As we stated in Chapter 1, college trustees are often fervent champions of change, and they usually assume that role as an antidote to a perceived antipathy toward change on the part of faculty and staff. Yet, trustees are, in general, as conservative about self-reform as any other campus constituency. Boards have deeply ingrained structures, routines, and habits. Many are stubbornly reluctant, for example, to alter the frequency and format of board meetings, the organization of trustee committees, or the channels of communication with major stakeholders. Even greater numbers resist "newfangled notions" like retreats, fast feedback, prioritized agendas, and trustee mentors. "That's not how we do things around here. We always . . ." explain the defenders of the status quo.

To be successful, boards must create a climate conducive to change, and we believe that can best be accomplished through experimentation. Too often, trustees act as though any changes in the way the board does business must be permanent and irrevocable. A change need not be forever; board development can be approached through trial and error. Effective boards experiment; they retain what works exceptionally well, modify what works reasonably well, and discard what does not work. Over time, more trustees become more engaged in more issues of more consequence, and the board discovers better ways to govern so as to add greater value to the institution now and over the long term. And that, after all, is the essence of trusteeship.

REFERENCES

• • • • • • • • •

Alderfer, Clayton. 1986. "The Invisible Director on Corporate Boards." *Harvard Business Review* 64(6): 38–52.

Aram, John. 1996. "Corporate Governance: A Delicate Balance." *Strategy*. Cleveland: Weatherhead School of Management, Case Western Reserve University, January: 7–14.

Association of Governing Boards of Universities and Colleges. 1986. *Self-Study Criteria for Governing Boards of Independent Colleges and Universities*. Washington, D.C.: AGB.

Association of Governing Boards of Universities and Colleges. 1991. *Survey of Board Characteristics, Policies, and Practices*. Washington, D.C.: AGB.

Birnbaum, Robert. 1988. *How Colleges Work: The Cybernetics of Academic Leadership*. San Francisco: Jossey-Bass.

Birnbaum, Robert. 1992. *How Academic Leadership Works: Understanding Success and Failure in the College Presidency*. San Francisco: Jossey-Bass.

Bowen, William G. 1994. *Inside the Boardroom*. New York: John Wiley & Sons, Inc.

Butler, Lawrence M.; Gary B. Hirsh; and Susan S. Swift. 1995. *Board Information Systems*. Rockville, MD: The Cheswick Center.

Chait, Richard P. 1995. *The New Activism of Corporate Boards and the Implications for Campus Governance*. Occasional Paper No. 26. Washington, D.C.: Association of Governing Boards.

Chait, Richard P.; Thomas P. Holland; and Barbara E. Taylor. 1991. *The Effective Board of Trustees*. New York: ACE/MacMillan (first printing); Phoenix: ACE/Oryx (second printing, 1993).

Chait, Richard P., and Barbara E. Taylor. 1987. "Evaluating Boards of Trustees: Theory and Practice." Paper presented at the Annual Meeting of the Association for the Study of Higher Education.

Chait, Richard P.; Barbara E. Taylor; and Thomas P. Holland. Forthcoming. "A Typology of Non-Profit Boards."

Cohen, Michael D., and James G. March. 1974. *Leadership and Ambiguity: The American College President*. New York: McGraw-Hill.

Demb, Ada, and F.-Friedrich Neubauer. 1992. *The Corporate Board: Confronting the Paradoxes*. New York: Oxford University Press.

Donaldson, Gordon. 1995. "A New Tool for Boards: The Strategic Audit." *Harvard Business Review*, 73(4): 99–108.

Dressler, Catherine. 1995. "We've Got to Stop Meeting Like This." *The Washington Post*, December 31: H2.

Fisher, James L. *The Board and the President*. 1991. Washington, D.C.: American Council on Education/Macmillan.

Garvin, David A. "Building a Learning Organization." 1993. *Harvard Business Review* 71(4): 78–91.

Giamatti, A. Bartlett. 1988. *A Free and Ordered Space*. New York: W.W. Norton.

Hamel, Gary, and C. K. Prahalad. 1994. *Competing for the Future*. Boston: Harvard Business School Press.

Holland, Thomas P. 1991. "Self-Assessment by Nonprofit Boards." *Nonprofit Management and Leadership* 2(1): 25–36.

Holland, Thomas P.; Richard P. Chait; and Barbara E. Taylor. 1989. "Board Effectiveness: Identifying and Measuring Trustee Competencies." *Research in Higher Education* 30(4): 435–53.

Holland, Thomas P.; Barbara E. Taylor; Richard P. Chait; and Douglas Jackson. 1996. "Measuring the Performance of Governing Boards." Unpublished manuscript.

Jacobs, Richard O. 1991. "Why Boards Miss Black Holes." *Across the Board* 28(6): 51–55.

Kennedy, Donald. 1994. "Making Choices in the Research University." In *The Research University in a Time of Discontent*, edited by Jonathan R. Cole, Elinor G. Barber, and Stephen R. Graubard. Baltimore: The Johns Hopkins University Press.

Kotter, John P., and Leonard A. Schlesinger. 1979. "Choosing Strategies for Change." *Harvard Business Review* 57(2): 106–14.

Lorsch, Jay W. 1989. *Pawns or Potentates: The Reality of America's Corporate Boards*. Boston: Harvard Business School Press.

Lorsch, Jay W. 1995. "Empowering the Board." *Harvard Business Review* 73(1): 107–17.

Minow, Nell. 1994. "Do Your Duty, Retirement Managers." *New York Times* January 30: F11.

"Overhauling Paper Overload a Key to Better Board Work." 1995. *Trusteeship* November–December: 32.

Patton, Arch, and John C. Baker. 1987. "Why Won't Directors Rock the Boat?" *Harvard Business Review* 65(6): 10–18.

Pound, John. 1995. "The Promise of the Governed Corporation." *Harvard Business Review* 73(2): 89–98.

Schein, Edgar H. 1993. "How Can Organizations Learn Faster? The Challenge of Entering the Green Room." *Sloan Management Review* 34(2): 85–92.

Senge, Peter. 1990. *The Fifth Discipline: The Art and Practice of the Learning Organization.* New York: Doubleday.

Smith, David H. 1995. *Entrusted: The Moral Responsibilities of Trusteeship.* Bloomington: Indiana University Press.

Taylor, Barbara E. 1987. *Working Effectively with Trustees: Building Cooperative Campus Leadership.* ASHE-ERIC Research Report, No. 2. Washington, D.C.: Association for the Study of Higher Education.

Taylor, Barbara E.; Richard P. Chait; and Thomas P. Holland. 1994. "Trustee Motivation and Board Effectiveness." *Nonprofit and Voluntary Sector Quarterly* 20(2). Reprinted in *Management of Nonprofit Organizations,* edited by Sharon M. Oster. Aldershot, England: Dartmouth Publishing Company, Ltd.

Taylor, Barbara E.; Joel W. Meyerson; and William F. Massy. 1993. *Strategic Indicators for Higher Education: Improving Performance.* Princeton, NJ: Peterson's Guides.

Taylor, Barbara E.; Joel W. Meyerson; Louis R. Morrell; and Dabney G. Park Jr. 1991. *Strategic Analysis: Using Comparative Data to Understand Your Institution.* Washington, D.C.: Association of Governing Boards.

Ward, Leah Beth. 1996. "In the Executive Alphabet, You Call Them C.L.O.'s." *New York Times* February 4: F12.

Weick, Karl. 1983. "Managerial Thought in the Context of Action." In *The Executive Mind: New Insights on Managerial Thought and Action,* edited by Suresh Srivastva, 221–42. San Francisco: Jossey-Bass.

INDEX

•••••••••

by James Minkin